PERSONAL POET
of
GOD

ARTHUR KNACKMUS

Copyright © 2020 by Arthur Knackmus.

ISBN   Softcover   978-1-950580-71-2

All rights reserved. No part of this book may be reproduced or transmitted in any form or by any means, electronic or mechanical, including photocopying, recording, or by any information storage and retrieval system without express written permission from the author, except in the case of brief quotations embodied in critical reviews and certain other non-commercial uses permitted by copyright law.

The Bibles are King James Version and The Children's Version.

Printed in the United States of America.

To order additional copies of this book, contact:
Bookwhip
1-855-339-3589
https://www.bookwhip.com

Contents

Looking up to the Sky at Night 1
Clowns Butterfly's Dog 2
Why West Salem? 3
In The Beginning Our Lord Was Alone 4
Who Was the Wisest Ever? 7
Differences of Heaven and Hell 9
Thank God for God 10
Women Were Once Popes 12
Birds and Bees 13
A Hard Nut to Crack 14
I Am God 15
Jesus Talks to Me 16
Did the Angels have Guitars Before Wings? 17
A Game From Above 18
Right Wins to Write 20
Wise in Your Eyes 21
Sorrow Comes With Knowledge 22
What Time of Day Was It? 23
Life Styles of Poor and Depressed 24
What is Rich? 25
Rule the World 26
You Live in Your World—I've Got Mine 27
Nobody Told Me 28
Why Say Sorry? 29
Art You Are the Poet in My Heart 30

Satan's State	31
Satan's Rule	32
Dollars and Sense	33
Prisoners in This World	34
People Believe the World is flat and Square	35
It's Not Good to go Back in Time	36
Yes, For the Love of God	37
Compare U.S.A., Japanese, German Steel, Steal and STIHL	38
Too Common	40
Am I With the High Command?	41
The Stakes Were High	42
Keeping the Ten Commandments Does Not Get us to Heaven	43
In America We Have Freedom of Speech	44
Land of the Free	45
Justice the American Way	46
The Atomic Bomb Gift to the Jews	48
Broken Spirit	50
Monkey Business	51
Our World is Foolishness	52
War	53
Where Is the Love?	54
Life's Mistakes	55
Winners and Losers	56
The True God is Jesus	57
Earth to Me	58
Anxiety	59
Secret Societies	60
Future Communist	61
Anxiety 2	62
Giants	63
Writing Poetry	64
Everybody Wants to Rule	65

Say No More 66
Isn't This World a Joke? 67
Real Story 68
Should Be, but Don't Know after Educated 69
Due Process of Manufacturing 70
Angels are Given Last Revenge 71
Hope Like Hell 72
Just Can't Win 73
If I could Read Your Mind? 74
Everybody Works For a Government 75
I Have the Key 76
So Sad But True 77
How do We Stop Nuclear Fusion? 78
Describe the Man That Beat the Japs at War 79
Who is Better? Who is Best? 80
Gangsters Fables 81
The Family God Loves More Than Life 82

Biography 221

Looking up to the Sky at Night

1998

Looking up to the sky at night.
Why are there no stars shining bright?
Many times I have looked up for any stars light.
Just to see a total darkness and no stars that shine white.

Is this Gods way of telling us in Heaven there is a fight?
Over something simple does might make right?
We just have to submit ourselves to God and hold on tight.
Because we humans are in a world with a hopeless plight.

By now you know I am quite right,
That sometimes there are no bight, white, lights at night.
Yes, some stars are a little red or yellow depending on their energy, which is light.
And from this you can tell I have good eyesight.

It's not my intention to scare people into a fear or fright.
About this matter I've chosen to write.
No matter who you are eventually you will go through blight.
Even if you are King Arthur or a white knight.

In this small town an angel could show the height of his flight.
Amazing you at night going higher than a kite.
This world is just a play and West Salem is God's chosen site.
Please pray that in Illinois everything will be all right.

Clowns Butterfly's Dog

Last night, why was the Big Dipper upside down?
I think the angels, through God, control the universe in my town.
Are the angels at war or just showing of being clowns?
Hebrews read backwards, so God to them in English is just a hound. (Dog, God).
Other clowns in my town…to call God a hound
Would be a compliment to Him I've found.
So to them, Jesus should be gagged and bound, tied up in rope all around,
Then put to slave labor, like Samson going round and round.
I have found Jesus knows everything, everybody, and could weigh the universe to the exact pound.
Some people think they know anything, anybody, then say the world is sound.
The way Jesus runs the world is by winding it up and then its wound.
Before things happen, He can predict and synchronize every sound.
God is omniscient, omnipotent, and omnipresent, meaning Power, everything and surround.
He has power to spare and leaves you clowns down to abound.
He can think up new adjectives, verbs or nouns
Leading Him to define Him out in town.
You clowns never will, otherwise, you would be God the Hound

Why West Salem?

Why is West Salem so important?
All it's doing is holding the world together.
To God everything unimportant needn't be there.
People pass through this town with a frown.
Or laughing as being tickled with a feather.
Even though they are sitting in a car on leather.
Here, everybody does really like the weather.
Except during winter, spring, summer or fall.
Meaning not at all.
There isn't a thing here at all.
Not even the first shopping mall.
West Salem is a farming community,
People here only invest in annuities.
This community is stricken with poverty.
The only place to work is the one factory.
Money is tight here.
You can't even buy beer.
Or shoes shirts and pants to wear.
There is absolutely nothing here.
Not even a hog or steer.
It' said, "The factory, called Champ, is moving out next year."

In The Beginning Our Lord Was Alone

1998

In the beginning our Father was alone wanting company.
So to Himself He said, "I'll just create friends to suit my fancy."
They will all be Holy angels having freedom of choice.
Those Holy angels will be perfect in beauty having a voice.
All these angelic beings will have wings to fly away.
But I will set boundaries and limits where they are to stay.
They will also have eyes to see where to stop.
With ears to hear praises from the top.
By now the angels were given the sense of touch.
To the hierarchy in Heaven 'twas loved very much.
This sense of touch could be the feel of the wheel.
Boy what a deal.
And among other things could be pleasure,
This pleasure with God's measure,
Was their treasure.
All these spirits were given a mind.
Expecially being kind.
Possessing abilities to voice their choice.
Think at a blink, even wink, not blind.
Hear with ears even from behind.
The rank of the Cherubim was made of winged little girls and boys.
These cherubs walked and talked with God who gave then toys.
The boys played with balls.
The girls played with dolls.

These cherubs were happy, being content with all.
God was pleased with what He saw.
God gave all angels senses of smell and taste.
Instructing them they could lick in haste.
But never to taste paste or waste.
God gave angels given knowledge.
This a sixth sense not taught in college.
The wisdom acquired.
Will be required.
If so desired.
So stay chaste,
For the chase,
Being eternally chased.
At this time there was no sin, which is vice.
Everything in Heavens chorus was joyous and nice.
Our Father is Perfect so He didn't have to think twice.
He made no mistakes that couldn't be corrected.
When creating He got exactly what He expected.
Through His perfection is why God is always respected.
Everything God created,
Never became outdated.
He could raise His finger,
To invent some timber.
Or blink an eye creating the sky
That perfect magic Man could make something,
Simply out of nothing.
God created no two things exactly the same.
A female angel by nickname,

Was called dame.
God could create showers.
For all the flowers.
What was left of the rain.
Ran down the drain.
After these showers.
The man took to the dame.
As a gift, these flowers.
For the main spirit game,
Was to win the dame.
Then your spirit life and her name.
Would never be the same.

Who Was the Wisest Ever?

March 1999

King Solomon was the wisest man to ever live.
Outside of Jesus Himself.
Nobody on earth will ever be as wise again.
In the Old Testament Jesus offered Solomon anything he wanted.
What Solomon requested was knowledge.
Instead of wealth.
So Jesus gave Solomon both.
Immeasureable knowledge first.
Then the money and possessions next.
Now it's 1999; King Solomon lived thousands of years ago.
How could thousands of years ago, Jesus say,
Till the end of time
Solomon will be the wisest human ever to live?
He's God, so He done knew.
Lots of humans throughout their life.
Thought they were real brainy.
Why doesn't Jesus bring Solomon back up?
To see if the former king can compete with modern knowledge.
The man wouldn't even have to go to college.
He would say you couldn't tell me a thing.
Because I done knew.
Under the sun there is nothing new
Solomon would say over 4000 years ago
God drew me a picture.

Of the schematics of all future computers.
In heaven computers are obsolete.
As using a crank.
We have much better toys.
Computers aren't used up here.
They are collector's items.
Collected in yards we call junk.

Differences of Heaven and Hell

Sinners in Heaven are forgiven.

Sinners in Hell are unforgiven.

Angels in Heaven can't be perfect.

Angels in Hell have no salvation.

The Titans in Heaven are for good.

The Titans in Hell are for evil.

Lucifer ruled some angels in Heaven.

Now the former Lucifer, Satan, rules angels in Hell.

Everything in Heaven bows to Jesus.

Everything in Hell bowed to Satan.

Heaven is up.

Hell is down.

People forgiven in heaven are healed.

People unforgiven in Hell kneeled.

Heaven is spelled HEAVEN.

Hell is spelled HELL.

On earth Hell tells people what to do.

In Heaven, it knows everything telling Hell where to go.

The same God rules both places.

Every knee bows to the same God regardless of location.

Note: #1. Satan is the god of this evil world.

#2. Satan is not GOD.

Thank God for God

The time of the end of the world as we know.
Is only known by our Father in Heaven above.
You see there is a fallen angel named Satan below,
That man's evil spirit is the cause of loss of love,
Here and Above
We have to read Revelation.
That book even reveals the fate of our nation.
Everyone's fate depends upon God's plan,
To save the race of man.
So if you can.
Read and reread the plan.
Revealed to Brother John our man,
God's case,
Of free grace.
The war in Heaven caused the fall of the angels
Satan is the leader of these fallen angels.
God Almighty gave eternal punishment,
As final judgment,
But to us humans have offered atonement.
This means no free grace to the fallen ones.
Unforgiven, because they were the cause.
So Michael kicked Lucifer and 1/3 of the stars from heaven to earth.
These angels that fell to Hell, called earth.
Knew well they deserved Hell.
The Michael I mentioned here does not mean the angel Michael,
But is meant to be Jesus.
Who said He would not leave us.
Lucifer was the greatest angel created.
Now he will always be hated.

His name meant opposite of night,
Which is light.
When Lucifer was created, he was perfect in beauty and a signet of perfection.
This, with his pride, led to his defection.
To tell about the former greatest archangel.
Is to say he is the Devil, so we need protection.
This world on earth is Hell to me.
A synonym of earth is Hell for me to see.
This world needs protection.
With Divine direction.
To save us from the man of perdition.
Some can't see.
The good angels that did not sin within.
Now being called the Elect.
Are the ones God left to protect.
Jesus could have destroyed sin,
Before it even began.
He wouldn't even destroy the ones who sinned time after time, again and again.
Total annihilation would make the Elect live in constant fear.
Year after year.
Throughout time, the fear of more sin, within.
Would be a constant reminder of an angel who had been.
God promises in due time there will be war no more.
He will settle the score.
Does any of this make sense to you?
Or is it all taboo to you?

Women Were Once Popes

1999

Three times a Pope was a woman.
Instead of a man.
Believe this if you can.
These women were cross dressers looking like men.
YES, three women were the leaders living ruling the Vatican.
Of course, each had a special plan.
Getting elected to the highest position in the world of man.
In the Vatican all women were banned.
Crafty women used ways to infiltrate the Vatican's secret clan.
In religion, women had taken all they could stand.
From men that don't understand women.
Back then, could you imagine being a lowly woman?
And having a High Class man manually using a fan.
With his hand.
To cool her off after she ran.
The powerful state, The Vatican.
Women Popes were the most powerful humans of all lands.
During their tenure, lacking the correct sex glands.
Arts not kidding about a woman leading The Vatican.
They, wishing He would shut up of women Popes faked as men.

Birds and Bees

1999

What about the birds and bees?
There aren't any that I see.
This boy in Illinois.
Thinks that is a little strange during July.
Because we are missing the winged ones that fly.
The bees are dead, but why?
The birds come and go, so they did not die.
It's 1998 do you people think I lie?
Maybe stretch it a little if ii try.
'Cause yesterday someone said he saw one bee.
That would also seem strange to me to see just one bee.
If people were allergic to a sting they would be happy.
To see nary a bee.
When near a flower or fruit tree.
But these same people would miss the birds if only they knew they flew away.
I have known since ten years ago last May.
That in Illinois all birds flies away in May.
Leaving this area during summer for several days.
Blame me, am I the one that has to pay,
For no Blue Jay in the U.S.A.?

A Hard Nut to Crack

How can somebody,
Know or be anybody?
Cause the nobody to some isn't anybody.
But the nobody exists having a body.
If a body is nobody,
But still is alive of all things.
The alive thing has to be something.
Because the thing can't be nothing.
So we couldn't say nobody really isn't anything.
Would it be correct to say nobody has a body?
Would it be correct to say nobody is also nothing?
But then Mr. nobody has a body.
The body has to be something.
So how can an alive someone be nobody?
If nobody has a body.
That nobody surely is something.
Even if he is a nobody.
That nobody liked for anything.
And is also liked for nothing by nobody.
Nobody is nobody.

I Am God

1998

Will people know each other?
After we are dead and gone here after?
To several people this doesn't matter
They would assume frying like batter
That's rolled around the fish on their platter
People can be cold as frozen water
Hating their father and mother
Even their sister or brother
Do I have to draw people a picture?
That there is a heaven in the future
Each of us will know sooner or later
To know we don't need to be a teacher or preacher
We all will eventually sense feelings of a Savior
And His opposite who is an unforgiven deserter
This deserter is Satan or Lucifer
These two opposites aren't exactly lovers
Each is on opposite teams trying to be the winner
Who is going to be the loser?
Do we all know the devil Lucifer?
And Jesus our Savior?

Jesus Talks to Me

1998

Why does Jesus talk to me?
I think it was just meant to be.
For Him to take me out to tea.
And fly like a bird or honeybee.
By a lake or over the sea.
He said, "He could free me"
From all my sins you see.
From some the cost of grace is free.
Others must think they get by paying God a fee
Saving them from evil,
To be
In serenity
Throughout eternity
We are playing for to be forever happy.
Having a peaceful feeling called serenity.
Throughout eternity
With me, about eternity
Jesus isn't shy
Please, ask me why.
I guess I was too shy a guy.
In this world to get by.
So Jesus would try.
Before I would die.
And make my brain fly.
So I would not fry.
About a white lie.
Thus, never forever
Having to God say, good-bye.

Did the Angels have Guitars Before Wings?

1998

God chose me because the others wouldn't understand.
About Rock N Roll and God being a member of the band.
God is omnipresent meaning He is everywhere in the air, sea or land.
I think He knows everything even numbering the beaches grains of sand.
If we are good He will eventually lend us a helping hand.
Could make you a leader of one of His bands.
Some songs are bland,
Meaning God sometimes can't stand,
All the groups' music in every album of the bands.
Then some songs are so unique and very grand.
These songs are longed to belong in Heaven, ask the Tribe of Dan.
But some songs couldn't make it to the top 100 in this land
Not even getting on American Bandstand.
Sometimes missing simply because they had the wrong name on the label brand.
Or somebody did not get enough money placed into the palm of his hand.
Then maybe somebody quit or got canned.
From being a member of the lands potential #1 band.
Jealousy is a cruel as the grave, true in every land.
Read the Bible or ask any member of any lands bands.
I get my information from radio, the library and a bookstand.
I have read God numbers hairs on our heads in every last stand.
Please bands, don't tell me nobody told me AND …Etc.
Don't forget the fan.

A Game From Above

For a cherub the best game of all in Heaven was basketball.
Most members of the cherubim weren't tall they were small.
But in basketball they would excel leaving others in awe.
Holding the ball so they could put on a perfect stall.
The bigger and taller angels would dive for the ball.
Sometimes hitting the wall.
Or trip and fall
Breaking a jaw, while chasing the basketball.
When someone would fracture a jaw.
Or get hurt at all.
They would call their Father they also called Pa.
Pa would pick up the hurt one placing him in a healing spa.
Located north of our court called Assembly Hall.
The last time one of those cherubs hit the wall.
Was by a small cherub whose name was Paul Shaw.
Because of this injury, Father Pa
Ordered Assembly Hall,
To be lined with special shock absorbing straw.
Our Father saw He was going to have to make a law
Instructing officials to enforce safer rules and laws of basketball.
Pa said our game was turning into a brawl of sinful flaws.
Threatening to turn Assembly Hall.
Into a shopping mall
Or better yet, a livery stable with a stall.
For one of His white horses to be born this fall.
Sending everyone home to their teeter-totter or see saw.
Because He saw
What happened to the boy, Paul Shaw.
Was no accident at all.

Paul got a raw deal out of being purposely
pounded against the Halls wall.
Paul now can't even eat slaw.
Because of his fractured swollen jaw.
They guy sips everything through a straw.
Then he pouts a little bringing tears then he bawls.
He now has a fear of being chased with a splitting maul next fall.
By the angry guy now pretending to watch reruns of Jaws and Hee Haw.
With no hope of playing any basketball at all,
Till next fall.
Or until the poor guy recovers from his Assembly Hall fall.
The guilty one had to be punished, the lines Pa will draw.
From now on depending on the force of the fall.
The punishment will fit the crime every time in Assembly Hall.

Right Wins to Write

1998

125,000 of the Hebrew nation did not know the difference of left or right.
How then could one of them know how to read or write?
How then could they distinguish the difference between wrong and right?
Can you understand why they didn't get their spelling right?
If they couldn't even read or write?
Yes, there were philosophers back then.
They would ask does might make right.
Or ask then.
is sin
going to win
in the end?
The 125,000 were children.

Wise in Your Eyes

1998

If you think you are wise
In your own eyes
As a guiding rule
There is more hope for a fool.
This rule
Comes from a guide I read
While lying in bed
I just added the word Guide
So there is nothing to hide
But what about this one exception
Which may lead us into the right direction
Otherwise how could there have been an Immaculate Conception
Without this one exception
Did Jesus leave us?

Sorrow Comes With Knowledge

1998

You see our knowledge
Doesn't always come from college
Everything we know comes from above
By the God of love
The Bible says that he who increases knowledge
Increases sorrow
But many people will be off to college tomorrow
I bet your college doesn't teach knowledge
Of sorrow tomorrow.
The rule at school
Is don't be a fool
We need knowledge
So attend college

What Time of Day Was It?

Let's talk about sunlight or moonlight.
Each comes from the same stars light.
The sun and moon I will not slight.
Each we can see sometimes in daylight.
The moon our orbiting satellite,
Can usually be seen during the night
The main star, the sun is the origin of moonlight.
A few times the sun set fast before my sight.
To see the measurements wouldn't require a theodolite.
The sun moved down straight before eight.
For a few moments I could tell well by sight.
During daylight there was no sun for light.
No, I wasn't drinking a Lite not even Diet Rite or Sprite.
During this time there was no sun for light.
When our star goes below the western horizon way before night.
To me it would delight and excite.
Being 4:00 PM during daylight.
And no sun would shine bright.
Would it be daylight during night without sunlight?
Or night during daylight with light bright?

Life Styles of Poor and Depressed

I drove to town to keep my Doctors appointment for depression.

When we finished our discussion

He filled out my prescription

The Prozac helps anxiety and lessens tension.

Unless the patient has a bad reaction.

Causing him to lose control of his actions

The person with depression

Can lose interest in life even if owning a corporation.

Having a fraction of former satisfaction.

Needing to see a shrink for life's simple instructions.

The depressive patient couldn't do addition.

But if and when he comes out of his depression

God could make him smart enough to teach nuclear fission.

If that was his life's mission.

The depressive patient also can get hurt needing traction.

He will at least get some relaxation.

From the depression.

Inherited from his relation.

This type disorder runs in the family for generations.

It could ruin our entire nation.

The Doans Corporation,

Wouldn't have enough pills to fill the prescriptions

Without there being a national ration.

If everybody took their medication,

For depression.

What is Rich?

Rich is when everything is against you, but you still have one friend.
If the last friend leaves you, you'll be blue.
Because it's Jesus who stays till the end.
He is our King even if we're not Jew.
We have to depend upon Him to defend.
When it comes down to just two.
Everybody against two is poor odds to win.
But if you are half right also.
To you His Love will be true.
And you will win in the end.
To be a believer we don't have to sit in a pew.
A heathen can go to church calling you friend.
When coming down for him to show you he's true.
He will forsake you even in a church pew.
It won't be a surprise, you done knew.
Everybody acts as though they do not have a clue.
Of what's going on in this worldly circus zoo.
Or truly what to do for you.

Rule the World

How can I have a wife, in this life?
When life, is constantly strife?
Life is more strife.
Especially if you don't have a wife.
The Bible says Jesus is God,
He had strife.
I don't know if Jesus had a wife.
He was crucified promising everyone eternal life.
Jesus made the Garden of Eden having the Tree of Life.
In this Garden of Paradise.
Jesus made just one rule.
But Eve, being tempted by Satan's tools.
Was playing the fool.
Eve also ate from the Tree of Knowledge.
Now we have to go to school.
Attending college, for more knowledge.
But still some people don't know why there is life.
We keep fighting each other using a weapon or knife.
Saying no pain, no gain, by force we'll regain.
See God promises in due time,
A rebirth for the earth.
At death,
God will reward each of us, according to their soul's worth.
I will be content and wait for my date.
Receiving from God a wife.
After this earthly life.

You Live in Your World—I've Got Mine

1999

People always know they are right.
Just ask anyone if they are wrong or right.
The person questioned always agrees he's right.
And the person questioning disagrees, he's not right.
The disagreeable person gets answered with a left or right.
Because he's not right.
If both agree they are right.
Then no one is wrong but each right.
It's nice to know everyone is right.
With each disagreeing what is right.
All these disagreeing people who are right.
Will agree the others are wrong instead of right.
If nobody is wrong but right.
Who is left of Right?
When the wrong is turned to right?
If we people are fighting for right.
Who is left of Right?
If right is right of Right?
Our Father in Heaven is left of Right.
If Jesus is Right,
Are all we right humans on the left or right?

Nobody Told Me

Sept. 1998

I don't see anything
I don't hear anything
I don't repeat anything
I don't know anything
'Cause I know nothing
I don't see nothing
I don't hear nothing
I don't repeat nothing
'Cause nobody told me a thing
Then I don't know a thing
I don't see a thing
I don't hear a thing
If something happens to anything
I might know something
But know nothing about anything
Please don't ask me anything about nothing
Even if something happens to nothing
'Cause like I said I don't know a thing
And anyhow if I was told anything
I wouldn't at any time know anything about nothing

Why Say Sorry?

In this story
We don't ever say we're sorry
Because it's been mostly our worry
Facing the law and jury

Some people assume they are always right
Just ask the right people tonight
And I will guarantee you'll get into a fight
Because they think they have all God's might

I just might be God dear
And God people fear
From what I hear
God is always near here

Every guy thinks he is the greatest man
He, never realizing God gave each man a hand
Now knowing God owns all the land
Whether it's a clay hill or sand
We are God guys
Now, most everyone wants to fly
Some say why try to fly
'Cause they've broken every rule purposely, a lie Bye

Art You Are the Poet in My Heart

Why did you all?
Put me in the Hall?

The one Hall for poets of fame.

My poems are a little raw.
Breaking many rules of poetry law.

The Hall must have liked my name.

And by next fall
I'll be poet of the year.
Mainly on my poem about fear.
I'm waiting for the phone call.
From the Library of Poetry out east.
I have faith the phone will ring off the wall.
Even if I do not win first.
Losing in a dead heat draw.
Art still wants his poems published just the same.

To be poet of the year I'm way too common.
If winning meant all then I would be Mammon.
It really doesn't matter to me.
But I would love to win in Washington D.C.
Put the blame on wanting my name for fame.

Satan's State

Satan will make you late
For a date
The Devil is the god of hate.
You see I dwell
Because Satan fell.
You and I know darn well.
Evil Satan is in Hell.

Meanings are Sometimes Twisted
Sometimes in the Bible the opposite is meant.
And we can't tell the true meaning if Heaven sent.
You see I went sent and ate a mint scent.
How is someone that bright know about atonement?

Satan's Rule

The Devil's goal,
Is to steal every soul
From the God above
Who is the real God of love
Satan is the chief demon
He is always a schemin'
He will tempt us to sin
Thinking in the end he will win

Dollars and Sense

1998

Many people go to their grave doubting God's existence.
Even though they were Christian in past tense.
And toward evil the devil and sin had a low resistance.
But when they would get off the beaten path they want mercy, aren't they dense?
Arguments are just over someone's ignorance and dollars and cents.
Back to the root of all evil it is loving money with lack of sense.
Some arguments are over the lines of a crooked fence.
Since some farmers leaves a 50 ft. strip on each side of their fence.
It's because the judge wanted each farmer to keep his distance.
That's what happened in this particular instance.
Each would argue in court increasing his persistence
and try to change the fences distance.
The judge could change his mind changing his stance.
This would give each side a fair chance.
To change it's made up mind while at the next barn dance
Trying to work it out amongst themselves with each other's insistence.
Some people know everything fighting over a crank or three pence.
They wouldn't give you 2 or 3 pennies called cents.
If you don't have cents to give I understand, but why be in a trance?
Life is just a dance.
Pray to Jesus to give you some sense.

Prisoners in This World

March of 1999

Anything living is subjected to Satan.
In this evil world
Of pain, heartache and sorrow.
Earth is in the power of the Evil One today and tomorrow

If those words above are not true.
Then Jesus wasn't King of the Jews.
He, being God who we humans worship.
Allows this evil to exist.
So people will know good from evil, He insists.

We're taught in schools we can be anything we want.
I can be, if the Lords a willing and the creek don't rise.
Sometimes God gives us a surprise
When God gives us our ability talents, we're wise.
As Americans each knows there is no hope or cause to live if we are atheist.
Why do we Americans believe we are above others?
Just because God gave us special powers?
Here someday, somebody will get the bright idea again, constructing a tower.
Up to Heaven to get the rest of God's power.
People do not know we are God's PUPPETS. (wanna be a flower?)

People Believe the World is Flat and Square

1999

Jesus claimed to be God
The Jews don't believe Jesus is God
So the Jews crucified Jesus who is God
Both the Jews and Christians believe in God
Today most Christians worship Jesus as God
But the Christians say Jesus wasn't God
The Devil worshipers worship Satan as God
If Jesus wasn't God.
Then Jesus wasn't God
If Jesus wasn't our God
Then Jesus is the Devil worshiper's god
If Jesus is the Devil he can't be God but is Satan who is god
The Jews justify crucifying Jesus.
Because, He, Jesus, said He was God
How can Devil worshipers be anti-God? (Antichrist)
If an Antichrist doesn't even believe in a God (atheist)
People that are Antichrist believe Jesus was an imposter playing God.
If Jesus wasn't God.
Just playing acting God
Then He was the devil as God

It's Not Good to go Back in Time

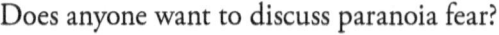

Does anyone want to discuss paranoia fear?
Let me then ask during what year?
We will start in the year 1940 with the fear
This should make it clear.
To most, because they have also had tears
From fears
Year to year
Some people to relieve their fears
Will resort to using drugs, Everclear or drink beer.
Then end up losing the ones they love so dear
Which just leads to more tears
Year after year
Also increasing the fear
That leads to drinking more cheer
F.D.R and Churchill each said, "We have nothing to fear but fear itself."
Those statesmen quoted this from a black book that usually sits on a shelf.
Of course it's Bible verse being God's quote of Himself.
It's easier to relate to schitzo fear if reduced from a giant to an elf.
And during war over here.
Workers would grind on a gear
To be installed in a tank or truck be used over there.
People over here and there would read and hear
About Blood Sweat and Tears
Over there and here
The winners get to throw confetti and cheer
The winners also bow again to say another prayer

Yes, For the Love of God

I saw a homeless helpless man on the street corner.
He handed me a hat and said "Please help me."
I pitched in to give him a break.
He sued me the next week.
I WENT BROKE THE NEXT YEAR
Driving home one night I saw a man lying along the road.
Watching him he was waving and hollering, "Help me."
I screeched my car to a halt.
He sued me the judge said, "Guilty."
I DON'T DRIVE ANYMORE
Walking to grocery store one night I heard a woman say, "Help me."
With two different types of guns she had been raped.
Someone found a pistol registered to me.
She said I'll say you're OK, others said no way.
So the state sued me because the gun was mine.
I SERVED TIME FOR SOMEONE ELSE'S CRIME
Standing by the Pool Hall, someone was pushed by a bully.
Before his head smashed the concrete sidewalk he screamed, "Help me!"
The bully ran off, the court said I was an accessory so press charges.
I SHOT THE BULLIES

Compare U.S.A., Japanese, German Steel, Steal and STIHL

Japanese steal as in stolen, is sometimes different than American steal.
When Japan steals on any deal.
Their measurements weigh less when buying by real steal.
A ton of Japanese stolen steel.
Weighs about three pounds more than Americans stolen steel, so to an American steal gimmick deal.
You've stolen less per ton compared to a Japanese gimmick to steal.
Germany had several STIHL ® saws made of combined Jap & American steel.
Needless to say the STIHL ® saws were eventually acquired by Jap steal.
The Japs by computer would steal the saws made by STIHL ®
Out of this combined imported steel.
This way the Japs could sell STIHL ® saws cheaper by way of U.S. steal.
In turn, the American could sell the cheaper German STIHL ® saws cheaper than Germany could by Jap steal.
The Japs have earned all the American steel mills
So America only has Jap steel.
Americans to deal, in the metal steel, has to go through Jap steal.
Some say Japanese steel, is plastic steal.
American steal and Japanese steal, could be the same if all the saws are STIHL ®
Or then the German made STIHL ® saws would be American steel.
By way of Jap steel.
Let's get real.

For some reason when America sells American steel.

It weighs more in the USA than when weighed by Japanese Steel.

In Japan is that steal?

And when we Americans buy back the former American stolen steel.

Even that steel, weighs less per ton on a wheel. So we Americans will receive back less of our former exported steel.

Cause we did not pay in full for our steel.

Or for the saws from STIHL®

Who are the biggest wheeler, dealers, and stealers of steel?

Most people know about lead, which is real German steel.

Too Common

1998

I get the feeling we are living in the past.
For the night before last.
The memories were being scanned fast.
Of the future not the past.

If the memories are of the past future,
Then the future has done past.
And the future is just the past
Even though it was just a dream of the future

Has the dream already happened?
Because you've seen it in a dream?
But it is yet to be.
If someone has seen something.
Then to me,
If we dream of anything,
And later it happens becoming real reality.
Was the dream a dream or reality?

Still we can't prove a dream until it becomes true.
But then you knew.
So is the real reality new?
If we done knew,
Reality can't be new.

Even though we know.
Dreams haven't become reality

Am I With the High Command?

1998

The Good Book says nobody is good but God.
I am a Jew so that makes me a no-good Jew.
A person should believe in God, many do.
The Jews were God's chosen few.
They were contrary and hard necked too.
To learn being the least of people is nothing new
To a Jew.
We few, don't believe Jesus is God not having a clue.
Who God is, but to a Christian, that God Jesus is ewe.
Ewe meaning Lamb of God who forgives you.
For whatever you do.
Me being a no-good Jew.
I feel, I'm wasting my time sitting in a church pew.
Especially if our forefathers crucified the main Jew.
Making our loving God blue.
Giving Him pain as in practicing voodoo.
As Jews, we are still waiting for our Messiah, He's past due.
Every morning I wake up feeling like an unforgiven Jew.
For causing hurt to God Jesus.
The too perfect Jew
I suffer to.
Do you?
Jesus, counting you suffering to.
That makes at least two, who do.

The Stakes Were High

If we were sent from Heaven to earth by the High Command.
From us what would you ask for or demand?
Would it be wealth the Stealth or health?
Or would you try to cut our throats?
Then to everybody do gloat and bloat?
They know who we are in this place.
But they will not listen to words from my face.
People pray daily to God saying their grace.
But secretly amongst them running a race.
Thinking they're an ace.
And there won't be anything left of us to leave a trace.
The Bible says every dog has its day.
We've been dogs from day to day.
Having to pay.
Everybody makes mistakes, even the angels who can fly away.
Enough is enough; please tell people they follow Satan's sway.
And the only way,
We can get to Heaven is through God's free grace.
If people only knew, to God, we humans are just a disgrace.
Jesus was sorry He made humans to replace the fallen angels here.
Because the human heart is continually evil, that's clear.
If anybody doesn't have an ear.
Please God let those deaf hear.

Keeping the Ten Commandments Does Not Get us to Heaven

If a person said he kept all the Ten Commandments.
He has already made himself out a liar
Giving him NO CHANCE of getting to Heaven.
To receive total atonement forever
With our Lord Jesus.
The Perfect Christian God.
If a person says he broke all but one of the Ten Commandments.
That person is still a liar.
Because the Bible says, "Broke one you broke them all."
So still to God the person speaking is a liar.
Disqualifying that person from entrance to the place of Salvation.
Everybody agrees, the Bible says liars go to Hell.
This is according to all truthful Christian believers
If people are Christian and do not believe in the Ten Commandments.
They are still sinners being sometimes as bad as the ones believing.
In these Ten Laws delivered by God's angels to servant Moses.
One Commandment is (THY SHALL NOT LIE)
Obeying this rule does not get anybody to Eternal Life.
Rules, laws and regulations only condemn us who sin.
HOW DO HUMANS GET TO HEAVEN, EVEN THOUGH THEY THINK THEY KEPT GOD'S LAW?

In America We Have Freedom of Speech

March 11, 1999

All Americans have freedom of speech.
As long as they will do nothing about anything without money.
Where money is involved verbal expression of one's self could be manually.
By using secret signals with hands fingers or whatever
To get that extra crooked, self-made, hard earned dollar
People think the Constitution gives us all justice.
Until they must give in to Americans unjust JUST system of justice.
Ask anyone if an American cheated him or her legally.
Everybody agrees they've been screwed
Being fools like the rest
Ask a slave
Ask a factory worker.
They all know people get the shaft.
In every craft.
Including the craft that invented the shaft.
How do we meet someone half way?
Especially when it comes down to one aborted fetus?
America needs to stay stupid compromising
And have courts making decisions cutting fetuses in half.
Thus, making all parties equally one half happy.
SOME PEOPLE ARE NEVER PLEASED IF WE GIVE IN MEETING THEM HALFWAY.

Land of the Free

Japs hate Americans because they got their land free.
America being a land of freedom of the free was free
That's why America is called land of the free.
The land in the U.S.A. just sprang up the taking was free.
Others could not compete with a country that's free
Americans claim nobody wanted this land for free
The price was a dollar and a quarter per acre if bothering to pay the fee.
Some paid this fee for the free land in a saloon ran for free
Not getting the title-correctly filed losing the fee
Thus, someone in the free saloon got his paid for land free
This price was like giving America away for free
After settlers incorrectly paid the lands fee
Giving away their paid for land for free.
It is hard for other countries to compete against a land this free
Overseas their citizens hate us Americans giving us a lot for free.
Free enterprise to them is a despised monopoly freely paying the fee
Not receiving the commodity from the free after paying the fee.
Other countries do not like countries that free.
The poor people overseas can't see
How we Americans openly advertise everything you buy is free
The more taken out the more is free.
Yes, free in America is a well-used synonym us being free
Exactly, that's what America advertises; "It's Free"
PEOPLE WILL ACTUALLY BELIEVE THE CONTITUTION AFTER INTERPRETING 100 TIMES 100 DIFFERENT WAYS WITH 100 DIFFERENT DECISIONS
Free is advertised freely in this priceless country.

Justice the American Way

March 18, 1999

Cities today go by the Old West rule,
Shoot the criminal yourself not going to court.
But when individuals carry out the swift justice practice.
The same people are against this swift justice practice.
Calling justice murder.
Needing extensive court proceedings they said they were against.
People say a murderer doesn't need a trial.
Because murderers are already guilty of murder.
If accused of a capital crime.
And a citizen carries out swift justice on his own.
By killing someone that committed a capital crime,
Then the person did the state a favor by getting rid of a serious criminal cheaply.
Swift justice carried out by a citizen is usually murder prosecuted by our state.
The same people wanting swift justice in our system.
Are usually against swift conviction that they request.
People bitterly complain about the legal system being slow.
But when people do it themselves it is not legal, needing a trial for the now
Accused criminal who killed a criminal unconvicted but guilty.
Why can a government kill people for a crime that was justly justified? But
Not being legal according to laws they believe in?
If a person is a murderer it's against the law to punish him even if he is guilty.
How many people in America are not criminals?
According to the laws in our country?
If all laws were enforced equally in all levels of our country's governments.
Against all individuals at any time equally by God.

America would not exist as we know it because everyone would be locked up in jail or BURNED.
Nobody would be here eventually to bitch and bellyache of others.
Then everybody living here would be happy including God.
Because God carried out his laws against all the American criminals that needed swift punishment by righteous justice judgments.

P.S.   THE REASON GOD DIED ON THE CROSS IS BECAUSE HE DID NOT HAVE A REASON TO LIVE ANYMORE. So God had his own church kill Him carrying out His plan

The Atomic Bomb Gift to the Jews

10% Fiction

When Albert Einstein was twelve years old.
God gave him secret knowledge to split atoms.
Albert promised God, only to use this powerful destructive force on America
At this time he had never heard of a Nazi allied with a Jap.
He only had views of Jews crap.
While other used a computer to figure.
How to make atoms split on paper.
He had already had atoms slitting for years.
He found, when they start splitting.
Sometimes he could not stop the process in the bin.
The only end is when the world ends
Otherwise the splitting lasts eternally.
The atomic bomb Albert finally showed America to design.
Is smaller than a firecracker compared to a star.
He did not want the splitting to last too long or far
If the fire lasted like at first he could make a star or quasar
Because of this many times Albert would plan to resign
His most important post with intelligence.
To himself he said the secret formula is mine
Against America Einstein had a grievance
Why would I help a country against us?
Albert finally gave in for us to win.
Saying drop one of these firecrackers on a Jap.
So Russia won't invade West Salem and Bone Gap.
With the A-bomb the war of Bone Gap against a Jap.
Was abruptly ended so on the map Bone Gap now owned the Japs.
Russia then declared war against someone blown off the map.

They, now part of the Union governed by Washington D.C.
When the Russians declared war against the defeated Japanese.
Was it a war against the defeated country.
Or the bent American knees?
American knees
Promised Albert's Jewish relatives
Land they would call a new country
Jews bought their country
With the Help of others power and money
Albert's Jewish friends are the Israelis.
Each wants the other to bow bend or be on their knees

Broken Spirit

April 18, 1999

Many times I've cried during the night.
Crying myself to sleep till daylight.
Schizophrenia, paranoia and fear were from God's might.
People, can be so cold to God's chosen no matter how bright.
The main ones who think they are bright of God's might.
Might have lost sight of right.
Now we have a major war to fight.
In light of the fact of who's right.
America now has a hopeless plight.
Of continuing helping others who might not be exactly right.
When money is getting tight.
God had received no pleasure and delight.
Of pain caused to the whites.
At His chosen site.
Lots of people should be paid to just go fly a kite.
Instead of having an honest job stealing the widow's mite.
War here, war there, who cares? I might.
It's too late to say sorry, call in the White Knights.
To fight a war with an end angels can recite.
Nobody cares. I don't care about myself tonight.

Monkey Business

Seems as though locally there is a lot of money business.
Lacking the necessary number of monkeys.
People will do anything to sell us out.
Apparently they don't have anything else to do.
But unknowingly to them, with God, play fools.
Some of these fools are so jealous of our family.
To God and us his or her sins are so bad making everyone sad.
Sins accumulating more and worse than dads and mine.
These fools now know to God they've become unforgiven.
So they have increased continually their evil activities.
Being so wickedly unremorseful that God doesn't want them around anymore
Neighbors have given up totally of being repented Christians throughout the remainder of their lives.
Continually cursing God Almighty's perfect judgments.
These people now know they possess an unforgiven account with God.
Finding their time attending church is a moral waste
Misleading other good forgiven hell deserving sinners of the churches congregation.
Costing even them the very souls they are trying to save.
Some very educated people don't have a clue to the facts being lied about.
Their church brothers can't believe choice members of their church stoop so low.
One thing for sure ya can't fool God even on one of His bad days

Our World is Foolishness

To our Lord in Heaven, this world is nothing but foolishness.
By the way we breed.
By the way we feed.
By the way we need.
By the way things seed.
To the way we traded beads.
By the way we signed away deeds, traded for those beads.
Or by keying a reed, with a major in the lead.
To the way humans bleed, from an artery.
How a woman bleeds form where she had peed.
Or why a cowboy rides high on a steed.
And how all of us have greed.
As a driving need.
To how armies make the peasants flee.
With kings greed the main need.
No wonder why so many get hooked on weed.

War

As long as Satan rules earth.
We will have war.
War is Satan's way
Or getting more diamonds
And souls to play with.
When bad happens to good.
People ask where is God?
I know God is alive being here.
He disciplines
The ones who He loves.
God put us in a world of evil.
Ruled by the Evil One, Satan.
When evil overtakes us.
People will ask, why me Lord?
Most really not knowing why.
When bad happens to good.
In America we call it free enterprise.
Some people benefit off others misfortunes.
But God loves us.
In a world of evil.

(All evil works toward good in God's government.)

Where Is the Love?

None of the state's care for the others.
Counties within the states don't care for each other.
Cities within the counties don't care for each other.
Each side of a city doesn't care for the other.
School districts don't care for each other.
Families don't care for each other.
Families don't care for their neighbors.
Whites don't care for blacks.
Blacks don't care for whites
The South doesn't like the North.
The North doesn't like the South.
Republicans are against Democrats.
Democrats are against Republicans.
Others are against both.
Some are against all.
Yet some don't care at all.
What's right here is wrong there.
Divisions still exist today like yesterday.
Where is the brotherly love in America?
Nobody can stand anyone if they are truthful.
No matter what country they reside in.

Life's Mistakes

I SET THE WORLD ON FIRE.
Not knowing why, what, when or where.
No, maybe it was my brother, who set the world on fire.
I keep asking why us Lord?
Not one of us humans is perfect.
Whatever I've done I am sorry
Sorry is sometimes all I have to say
We are only humans we are supposed to make mistakes.
Some people just
make bigger ones.
The devil was God's number one man in command.
He was the highest-ranking angel of his time.
Where's he, what's Mr. Beautiful up too?
He also broke God's law.
The Bible says you broke one law,
You've broken all ten.
Remember laws only condemn.
They don't justify.
The purpose of life is, for God to show humans, the life they lead is wrong.

Winners and Losers

Sin causes pain.
Pain rids us of sin.
When sin leaves.
We'll have a real free world.
Back being perfect to God.
When we win over sin.
Pain will go with the sin.
Both a bad bad memory.
To God again and again.
Lucifer now rules earth with sin.
God will lock him up again.
Jesus will win in the end.
For our gain.
Of the riddance of pain.
Only Jesus knows when sin ends.
Ending Satan's rule.
Of all earth's fools.
When the world ends as we know it.
Some go to Hell with the sinful pain.
Others will be in Heaven, a peaceful Paradise.
Where Jesus took away all our sins and pain.

The True God is Jesus

A Christian is a forgiven sinner.
Forgiven by Jesus, who is the True God.
Problem number one is this.
Most Christians don't believe Jesus is God.
If a Christian doesn't believe Jesus is God.
How can Jesus forgive them of this sin?
I don't know if Jesus can forgive those unbelievers.
But Jesus is God in my Christian beliefs.
According to the Bible blasphemy is not forgiven.
And unbelief in the Christian God is blasphemy.
This unbelief is an unforgivable sin by Christian beliefs.
According to John Jesus made the world.
Nothing could exist without Him.
If Jesus isn't God to a Christian.
How can they have hope and faith of a true Christian?
Do these unbelievers have hope to the unseen God?
The Pharaohs claimed to exist?
If Jesus isn't God to a Christian.
They like the lost ones they make fun of.
Also have no hope.

Earth to Me

Earth can be a place worse than Hell.
Earth has been called the perfect world.
Earth was once proved flat and square.
Earth is round.
Earth was called Hell years ago.
Earth will be called Heaven in years to come.
Earth can be fertile and green.
Earth will be returned to a cinder.
Earth can be enjoyable and satisfying.
Earth can be miserable and depressing.
Earth goes in a circle.
Earth is deceiving.
Earth keeps turning.

Anxiety

Anxiety is a form of pain
It can drive us insane.
Along with paranoia, schizophrenia and fear.
I've had all these for years.
Driving me to tears.
These mental bugs.
Can be controlled with drugs.
If the dosage is correct.
If the dosage isn't correct.
You can become worse than not taking a drug.
Life is miserable with these mental bugs.

Secret Societies

Hundreds of secret societies are trying to rule the world.
Each wants to do it their way.
They want us to beg.
In the end they will own us
They will do away with Christianity.
Turning us to atheism.
Or force the people to worship Lucifer.
These societies have been around for thousands of years.
Some have secret powers, of ruling with secrets.
People don't know they help an evil society.
By being a member with a helping hand.
They will control each mind and lifestyle.
There are some good societies.
The good ones are no matches for the bad ones.
Someday people will wake up to find out.
The world will fall,
To the forces of evil Satan stands for.
To stop this the world needs to repent.

Future Communist

Disarmament is the United Nations goal,
To de-arm every nations military.
To de-arm every citizen.
In every country.
No one will have any weapon.
Except United Nations soldiers.
Leading to a one-world government.
Eventually foreign soldiers will be in America.
Guarding United States citizens with weapons.
Nobody will be able to protect themselves.
from the foreign soldiers on USA soil.
What's going to happen to the United States?
America will have to destroy or turn all nuclear
Weapons over to the United Nations.
Yes, the time is coming to dis-arm America.
Our government has already agreed to it illegally.
How can America have an army,
if all USA soldiers are UN soldiers?
And the United Nations is mostly communist.
For a one world government.

Anxiety 2

I used to be a poet
Until, anxiety set in my body.
Eventually prescribed Valium.
My mind is in wonderland.
Wondering what's next.
Anxiety is an awful feeling to experience.
It makes one want to wring his neck.
One can't sleep or get much rest.
Feeling unhappy and sad.
Eating dinner and lunch
is about the only enjoyment.
I lay here in bed trying to get relief
from this disorder of the mind.
But the anxious feeling only gets worse.
All I needed was three little white pills each day.
To stop my suffering leading to tears.
The treatments and answers are sometimes there.
But why does one have to suffer so long
When you've done been to doctors for help?

Giants

Giants used to walk the earth.
They were off spring of angels and human women.
God destroyed the world because of these giants.
They perverted everything God created.
The Nephilium told heavens secrets to humans.
They did the Devils work.
These cross breeds were cannibals.
They drank blood.
Giants did everything trying to rid man of God's grace.
The angels that left their proper dwelling,
are unforgiven to this day.
So these wondering stars are chained reserved in darkness.
They were walking in their own lust.
They were rebels of perversion.
They were changing the DNA pattern.
The offspring of the women weren't in God's image.
Man was placed on earth to replace the fallen angels.
The angels were jealous of man.
The giants claimed to be God.
Nobody knows all the evil: giants and angels did.

Writing Poetry

Writing poetry is a gift from God.
The poets God chooses.
They are sometimes for His benefit.
Helping Him spread knowledge.
Some people are born poets.
Others are made poets.
Some are neither made or born.
But like I said chosen.
A made poet thinks he got it on his own.
A born poet was master at a young age.
A chosen one knows God chose him.
All three can be the same.
Cause they were each chosen by God.
This gift from God can come easy.
Once you've been made a poet.
As easy as one that was born a poet.
The chosen poet's words maybe are found the hard way.
According to God's will.

Everybody Wants to Rule

Nobody likes to be told what to do.
Whether it's at home at work on the road or anywhere.
People wants to tell others what to do where to go or when it's done.
Some people are good at telling others what to do.
The others are forced to do it because of some, with money.
Money talks telling others what to do.
Unless the money is borrowed.
Then the money tells the borrower what to do.
Ruling is an ultimate goal.
But when reaching the goal of ruling more power is desired.
Which is the lust of more money anyway they can get it.
Whether it is somehow honest or borderline stolen.
In America our freedom laws help unlawfully in telling, some, what to do.
America's laws force honest people to do wrong.
Everybody wants to rule.
In turn, leading this world into a fiasco.

Say No More

Why doesn't the stars shine at night?
Why is the moon sometimes out of phase?
Why has the Big Dipper been upside down?
Why does other Heavenly bodies change their brightness?
Why are other Heavenly bodies in wrong positions?

I don't know the real reasons, but I have seen.
And I certainly am not a scientist.

Are people asleep or is what I see a little off base?
Maybe the angels are pressing the wrong buttons.
Angels controls the sun, moon, stars and etc....
Angels do as God instructs them to do.

If anyone has a problem, look up.
It, nice to me for God to show, proving Himself real.

Knowing of the real and true God, made life easier coping.
That is, if the Father forgives you.
I guess I am just a bad memory to the Godhead,
     my memory just never goes away.

Angels do magic all around us.
How long is Heaven going to be on fire?
Forgetting all this, will take a lot of time, for God.
Get the big picture?

Isn't This World a Joke?

Isn't this world a joke?
Everyone is nothing, but a hell deserving sinner, at best.
But many people think they are a lot better than others.
The love of money is the root of all evil'
    but money is the main way to measure ones success in life.
King Solomon said," life is useless," in the Bible.
Solomon also stated," life is foolishness to God."
I believe that wisest man ever.
People want to be King of the hill.
Yet we all have to look up.
Lots go to church, not knowing God really loves them.
Scientist made this world a joke
    because they know , having never seen.
People are so much more educated today
    though we still say don't know how.
Doctors and lawyers practice,
    yet they are professionals at their practice.
Laws are at times crooked, always have been, always will be.
People don't know much until they are charged or affected.
These are the two poem left out of the new book "Personal Poet of God"
Thank you for keeping them in this book.
I changed the wording some to make them better.
Arthur Knackmus the author
Isn't this world a joke

Real Story

America was populated because of religious freedom.
People wanted freedom from the church.
Some immigrants wanted freedom from the evil state.
Other words immigrants wanted to get far away from people.
Some because of the neighbors.
Others because of the crooked laws.
The Church would sometimes deport dissidents to the New World.
The Churches dissidents would then persecute the persecuting Church.
Then the persecuted Catholic Church members immigrated here to the New World.
They were unsatisfied being persecuted by their persecuted dissidents.
Thus, the persecuted on both sides ended up here in America.
Both sides were Catholic in origin.
Some members of the same Church have opposite beliefs
About being faithful to God.
This division still exists in society today.
But there is nowhere left to go.
Religion in Churches today like yesterday,
Is good only for arguments.
Maybe it's time for all us American Foreigners to go back home.
Turning America back over to real Americans the Native Indians.
God will sort us out in the end.

Should Be, but Don't Know after Educated

6/28/99

Students in schools should be dazed and confused.
Of what's right or wrong when told what to read and write.
If students aren't confused, they lack knowledge if out of college.
They are more brainwashed being misled the most of what's said.
Cause the church and state continually lies.
Of about anything especially if it's when we live or die.
To me education is supported the most by legal corruption.
Thriving on unsuspecting citizens ignorance of the real
worlds needed confessions.
The ones that have been disciplined by Christian thievery,
the most by our illegally run corrupt society.
Are usually chiseled down and broken down without the money.
Some not knowing why they are insufficient on funds, lacking money.
A politician that is less corrupt won't get many,
votes to win an election honestly being honored at his party's receptions.
If he does win the election honestly being honored at his party's reception.
Shortly after the election, the elected joins in this nation's corruption
Helping to direct this corrupt Hell run on deception.
Everyone knows how the world works leading nations into depressions.
Only telling children the way to real success is to stick their noses in a book.
But we can't always go by the book when it lies of the money each took.
A schoolbook doesn't try, to tell people God cries, of the nation's lies.
Asleep citizens can't relate until they die, then cry.

Due Process of Manufacturing

When a corporation
Decides to produce a product of production.
The procedure in this nation
Requires engineers of many professions with an education.
Here is the lesson.
After the factory receives the final draft to start production.
The product usually has to have flaws built in without detection.
So the production of the on purpose inferior product continues for workers job protection.
If a product would last forever there wouldn't be any legal production.
Of the product needing to be produced because nobody could squeeze a profit for their satisfaction.
To produce, it would cost too much due to the lack of demand.
So nobody could produce anything due to its perfection.
And the factory would shut down. Lacking enough orders to start production.
Also that's the result from raising the price from lack of sales.
Products like this being perfect just are not profitable in this nation.
We need corporations that make everything throw away the same day.
Nobody produces anything, sometimes due to the products perfection.
Even if we just worked one hour to produce the equivalent of what a whole shift did in a year.
If a person produced one item outlasting all the other same one million items.
Who produced the most?
Each of us has a job to continue production this way.

Angels are Given Last Revenge

July 1, 1999

God through His angels gets last revenge.
This is according to good Christian taught beliefs.
Today like yesterday, true Christians don't know what to believe.
Mostly they don't know what from whom to believe.
and never would believe the truth.
If anyone did tell them the truthful facts to believe.
Or especially if an angel of our Lord showed human truths.
A Jew, a Catholic, a Protestant and a Muslim,
Each has the same Old Testament teachings.
Exactly word for word down to the last comma and period.
In every sentence, paragraph, stanza and page.
Of all the books in the Old Testament.
If all four of these different religions differ one thing.
Then someone is wrong because they are taught the same Book.
Or someone is lying about what is being taught from the Bible.
These four differing religions that have the same Bible.
Will disagree on almost anything.
That is important or unimportant.
Leading me to wonder who is right or wrong in religions.
With each believing the same doctrines, yet fighting each other.
Whoever God is said to me, "You were the only one that knew Me at all."

Hope Like Hell

July 1, 1999

Hope like Hell
Jesus doesn't do to you
What He did to me
No I didn't spend time in a manmade jail
But loose in God's Hell on earth
Not suffering excruciating pain such as from a nail
But of another kind that never goes away
This type of pain hangs in there to stay
For consecutive weeks or a day
Never completely going away
Suffering sometimes for years.
Many times not being able to function, in tears.
With fears
Lasting indefinitely for years.
Sensing the worlds end is near
I now don't care the end is near
Each of us will receive his rightful eternal reward
As for me hearing this from the Lord
At times by way of a guitar cord.
While driving the old Ford
I'm back in the psycho ward.

Just Can't Win

7/10/99

A citizen improves himself.
His neighbor doesn't like new and improved neighbor.
Both are of Christian faith.
Improved neighbor always has to give.
New and improved citizen holds up for rights
Other Christian neighbors doesn't like new and improved neighbor.
Christian neighbor secret weapon against new and improved.
    (VASELINE)
Law sides with the side possessing Vaseline.
Sheriffs are puppets of States Attorneys.
Unless sheriffs tell States Attorneys what to do.
Many countries also have a Boss Hogg.
In addition to sheriffs and State Attorneys and hogs.
Most countries use this product Vaseline.
Money+law+more money+more money and power combined with Vaseline
    =LOSS
Some take it dry lie after lie.
Most have given up before fighting legal loopholes knowing they can't win.
from GOD; you guys are my inspiration.
from GOD; people can be so cold they will take your soul
Now ex improved citizen back to unimproved.
New unimproved citizen LOST being improved.
to GOD; why us Lord?

If I could Read Your Mind?

9/17/99

Wouldn't it be awful?
If a man could read all minds.
There are six billion hell-deserving sinners.
If only people knew
What's going through
Each of us sinners mind
Usually they'll always go against God
Whether the sinner is of the devil or Christian
I understand why people won't stand up for right
They want money and a job, cash is tight
Someone being good-natured
Is to be stomped into the ground the plays main feature
Kisses, payoffs, kickbacks and little cliques
That's what really makes our world go round and tick
Without evil corruption this world couldn't exist
People are weak unable to resist
Satan's power over greed, lust, power and jealousy.
It's an awful job to read minds of the devil

Everybody Works For a Government

1999

If an American citizen has a job.
His work is for our government.
If someone doesn't work.
Then our government works for him.
If the people our government works for.
Don't work for our government
Then those people works for other governments.
Whether they do or don't have a paying job.
Average American citizens curse our American government.
Not knowing the main reason for governments.
Is because the American people can't trust its citizens.
Americans simply can't be trusted.
The object of Free Enterprise is to make others busted.
Then a monopoly is created ruled by people consumers trusted.
Leading to the need for controlling governments.
The problem with government of America.
Is, it's the same people as the citizens of our country.
That couldn't be trusted, making others busted.
If people don't want to have a controlling government for their protection.
Give the government back rightfully to is civilian population no one trusts.
Government is suppose to work for the people.

I Have the Key

12/8/99

I have the key to God's heart.
My Earthly name is Art.
I was His choice from the start.
After the world was torn apart.
From the first ever war dividing Heaven apart.
Leaving earth formless and void, back to the start.
Yes, God had to start over again inventing the human heart
Now we lack atonement with God being apart.
From Him because of our evil human heart.
Earth was in CHAOS probably burned as a cinder
SATAN AND HIS FOLLOWING ANGELS HAD TO DEPART
Heavens war had to be stopped.
Or Heaven would be totally destroyed
By His angelic puppets,
In this muppet show, of powers regret.
After power is shown to get.
Leads us all to God an eternal debt.
That can't be paid without placing a bet.
That you are not stronger than He.
He won't turn His head, He will see.
Someone was paid off receiving a fee.
To see me on my knees.
BAD NEWS TO THE OTHERS OF MY KEYS…???!!
a king to be eternally

So Sad But True

Why do most women wear men's clothes?
But men can't women's clothes?
Why does a jock get to mock a woman not wearing a bra?
But a holes clothes when swimming must include the bra?
Why does a Joe and a Moe have to wear jeans?
But a Chloe or a Floe wears dresses or jeans.
If a guy dresses in a dress he is considered queer.
But is a girl takes off her dress and dresses in jeans she is in gear????

How do We Stop Nuclear Fusion?

Once the fusion is started
Atoms are starting to part.
The universes eternal division is restarted
This atomic energy.
Was several centuries in theory.
People figured til weary
Even till death
They will always bury the theory.
Until we have a better way to figure
Such as a computer.
In the thirties becoming reality.
Scientists were so afraid once division was started.
There was no switch to turn off, till all was parted.
In the real world the earth would turn to a star.
Or Quasar.
The world wouldn't be returned to a cinder
But consumed by eternal fire.
Leaving not a trace except gas, carbon and a lot of cinders.
We now have turned the world to fenders and cares, gas and ashes.
Parties and bashes. The Devil trashes mashes crashes. His stash.??

Describe the Man That Beat the Japs at War

He was created perfect in beauty.
He was a signet of perfection.
He is the Prince of the Power of the air.
The angels shouted for joy at his creation.
He was an anointed cherub. (now lacking salvation)
He wanted to rule the universe his way.
His war in heaven promoted him to god of this evil world.
People bow to worshipping him to get what they want (earthly power)
Nobody lives their earthly life without his touch.
He is a master deceiver being the father of lies.
He thinks he knows everything. (I think?)
Diamonds and souls are his greatest possessions.
His beauty and pride led to his downfall.
This evil shrewd man is craftiest at deception. (we're better off dead)
This victorious man is hated by everyone called righteous.
This tempter's evil spirit caused man's fall and exclusion in Eden.
SATAN, THE SERPENT ALSO CALLED THE DEVIL BEAT THE JAPS.
People say he has horns out his head. (not true unless in false pictures)
Congregations can't think at church lacking God's real knowledge.
Think I'm wrong? Go ask a church, a Jap. Or God, bring up Solomon.
Note: Fire is Satan's best friend.

Who is Better? Who is Best?

If right wins,
is the loser the winner?
Or is the winner the loser?
If wrong doesn't turn to the winning ways of another loser.
They the winners, losers to me also, while winning.
Still siding with a winning loser.
And if wrong is the winner.
Is right the loser?
If right has to join wrong, the winner?
Continuing doing wrong with the winning losers.
How can anyone be a winner?
Or are we all losers?
Being declared the winners, sometimes.
No matter which sinner won the war on sin.
A sinning Yankee can be the winner.
Or maybe a Yankee was the winner.

Gangsters Fables

Pushing my mind to the limit.
Here with nobody to love.
Where is it? The love.
I would love to the end.
Now I'm lonely to the point of hurting.
With not much crying.
Wishing I was hanging.
If bells aren't ringing.
Someday I will be found.
If not already.
My dreams are really cranky.
Me wishing for death.
With each breath.
Why do I have to suffer so?
When there are so many matches?
Maybe my world is make believe.
I wish to be relieved.
Please God, get the show on the road.
I'm about a brick shy of a full load.

The Family God Loves More Than Life

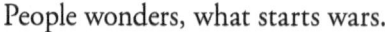

People wonders, what starts wars.
Sometimes it's a lawsuit.
Everybody help start wars, sue a Knackmus.
The last one was for millions.
It cost the states the Twin Towers.
Sue a Knackmus.
People in the United States really don't care,
about the fallen towers. Who cares?
I cried when I heard of another suit.
Knowing God was going to take vengeance.
Sue a Knackmus, come down towers
People really don't care soldiers die.
Sue a Knackmus.
People go to church and are the cause of wars.
Somebody done someone wrong.
Shakespeare, Milton, Knackmus
I ask God to be poet #3 to date.
Sue a Knackmus and God takes vengeance.
Yes I've made mistakes.
Art, I simply love you more than life itself.

Contents

Actually This World Produces Nothing 89
Agreeing is Believing 90
America the Ugly 91
Anyone Else Confused? 93
Are We All Equal? 94
As a Rule Gold Doesn't Always Rule 95
But They're Gonna Get a Surprise 97
Every Human has the Same Boss 98
Fair Game 100
Forgiveness 101
Get Even 102
God is in Control 104
God Wants Her Money Back 106
Good or Evil 107
I Can't Draw a Picture 108
If I Was 17 Again 109
Lonely Me 111
Loner in Town 112
Many Indians in U.S.A. 113
No Drink 114
Not Fed 115
Not Less: But More Miserable 116
Poet of the Year 118
She Will Take the Whole World Down 119
Shorts and Longs 120

Slaves to Satan 121
Takes One to Know One 122
The Best Days are Ahead of Us 123
The Blonde Bitch Next Door 124
Time Comes For Those Who Wait 126
War is Life in Fast Motion 127
What a Great Man He Was 129
What does it Matter? 130
Who Do We Send the Bill To? 132
Who Got Your Money? 133
Who is Responsible? 134
Who Says So? 135
Who Won? 136
Words to Me 137
Am I? 138
Fallen Angel's Second Chances 140
I Found the Devil 142
Money Thang 143
Strange 144
Teach a Peach 145
Poor Friend Shawn 146
Easy for You to Say 148
Every Knee Shall Bow to Me 149
Gangster 151
God Disciplines 153
History Speaks 155
Last Poem 157
Mission Control We Have a Problem 159
Prove It 161
Shoot Me, Drug Me, Burn Me and Bury 165
Turn the Other Cheek 168
What is it Worth? 170

Personal Poet of God	174
Hole in His Head	175
Why Believe?	176
A Free Country?	178
All Men Are Not Equal	180
Not Shy	182
Lottery	184
Imagine That	185
Print Truths!!!	187
Up and Down Limits	189
America Chose the Wrong Side	190
Unforgiven	194
Build World Around Me	196
Mercy, Mercy	199
See Ya N Hell	201
Cowboys, Indians, Negroes, Whites	203
Does Jesus Need to be Forgave	205
"The World" Brought to Its Knees	207
God is on Our Side	209
Legion After Legion of Angels	211
Vengeance or Mercy???	213
Use My Money	215
The End of Time	216
The Great Temptation of Jesus	218
Biography	221

Who Won

Actually This World Produces Nothing

Manufacturing like our farms really produces nothing.
They go by dollars and cents.
Not sense.
I knew that.

God gives each human a worthless job.
Some do not realize life's end result is death.
Until it's too late
Ending in a painful death because sin exists.
Does this painful transition to another world,
Leave us naked?
In the other worlds does God go by sense or cents?
To measure His subjects wealth?

To enter His house He offered each free grace.
Unless we paid Him off trying to buy His love.
Each farmer and factory worker
Comes from the bestest family in the world.
They are right because we are all brothers.
One person in town would not say this.
He lives in a fake dream world of his own.
Now knowing him and his buddies are eternal losers.
Look me in the eyes losers.
Tell me who the best friend of God is.

Like freedom the price of eternal life is high.
One you can buy.
The other one is eternal, called free grace.
Art, you are my bestest friend.
What did you produce at miserable work?

Agreeing is Believing

March 5, 2008

A Christian is someone believing Jesus is God.
An Infidel to a Muslim is someone believing Jesus is God.
Muslims want to rid the world of Christians or Infidels
All Christians do not believe Jesus is God.
Muslim leaders actually hate Christians.
Meaning they mainly hate Jesus, who is God.
The people in America that doesn't believe Jesus is God,
Shouldn't they be deported or executed for treason to U.S.A.?
They believe like, the people we are at war against.
If people agree with Muslims on this issue they are also
Against the U.S.A.
Other words the people unbelieving Jesus is God,
Are believing and agreeing with Muslim leaders.
That Jesus isn't God.
By this they commit treason.
Why is it people will deeply hate other people.
But agree with them on main issues of causes of war?
They will continually fight each other over these issues they agree on.
I have found, most people in the U.S.A. do not believe Jesus is God.
Why doesn't people here get together and please tell
The Muslim world, America agrees with them of Jesus.
Then there would be no reason to make war on Christians.
Because according to their Muslim beliefs,
They have already conquered us Americans and Christians.

Most of America says Jesus is not God and He is not innocent.

America the Ugly

God shows me the real world.
I, Arthur reads between all lines.
Sees the unseen in a mind.
Feels the unfelt.
Hearing what is left unspoken.

It's my opinion God is right.
Our United States is under Satan's influence.
Satan is ruling us.
It tastes salty.
Unknown to some Satan continues blinding minds.
Some not knowing what's been seen.
USA is living in a world of corruption.
Corruption is from the bottom up
All the way back down, to the top.
All we are, is hell deserving sinners at best.
Lack of perfection is the way God made us.
To be the most successful requires us to join
Professional theft and queer rings.
This before, during and after college.
Each wants to rule the world.
This world to rule, is called; tears for fears.
College students say they started with less than 0.
In all reality they are like me.
Could not add, subtract, multiply nor divide.
No wonder students flunk math.
They are not taught the correct math in school.

Saddam was right Americans are infidels.
An infidel to him is a person believing Jesus is God
Why doesn't a person know the facts?
start at 0 in multiplication and not end at 0.

This world will pass away for lack of knowledge.
Yes we all started at 0 or below.
God gives us all we have
We possessing what's all His.
I do not know what Jesus would do.
I know what He would say "JUST FUCK IT"
Who is Jesus going to send the bill to?

Anyone Else Confused?

Can nothing exist and
What would it look like if it did exist?

If God Died and all creation ceased
to exist upon His death.
What would the universe look like?
That is, if there was nothing in it at all?

If nothing existed in the vast universe,
Would death be a definition for nothing?

Would death cease to exist without a living God?
Where nothing could exist without God?
How could the dead be spirits in a universe of nothing?
If nothing could exist without our creator Jesus?
Assuming He is eternally dead?

If nothing existed how could anything be defined?
Where would the words come from?
Also who is to record them?

How could something start from nothing?
If nothing is there and everywhere in the universe
is nothing?
Where would this nothing from nothing come from?
If nothing existed in the universe?

Not even empty space??????

Are We All Equal?

12/2/07

Who loves God the most in Heaven?
It's the ones who are the least.
Other words the one's with the lowest number.
Having committed the worse sins.

The lowerst one will love God the most.
He's ranked last with the Holy Ghost.
The next step back was Hell roast.
He'll never boast the most,
because, in Hell he'll roast.

The Most High will also love the least most.
With lowly being chosen last.
By the Holy Ghost.

The number which is last.
Is first in Heaven's play cast.
He, having a blast.
God loves him at last.

Jesus has forgotten sinners earthly past.

As a Rule Gold Doesn't Always Rule

He with lead rules.
I now use a pencil, paper, eraser and ruler.
How many things contain lead?
Pencils, bullets, batteries, food, weights and battery leads.
Who owns deposits of lead?
Every country with a lead mine or a future mine.
(NOTE) Most are poorer states or countries.
Also everyone that buys from a lead mine owns lead.
Though it could be registered in another name.
Nobody knows for sure who owns the lead on the lien.
Most of the owners have gold.
Who has deposited lead?
The ones possessing it upon its return as a free flying gift.
If gold rules why does gold pay for menial lead?
Lead should be at least free, if one had enough gold to rule.
Leaders that have led nations into the lead with lead are:
Churchill, Roosevelt, Mussolini, Stalin, Hitler Lincoln
Hitler's country had so much money, burning it in stoves.
This was Germany's way of heating before Adolph came to power.
This heat caused him to turn it to lead.
(PAPER MONEY, POWER GOLD, THE COUNTRY)
Forcing others to trade gold for cheaper lead.
Both, receiving a returned deposit of ruin.
Seems such a waste to rule with paper turned now to plastic.
Knowing no gold backs it up
Paper is not always gold or lead.

'Cause like I said paper burns, but not like lead.
Gold rules with lead for protection.
On paper from paper,
Who is in the lead?
GOLD or PAPER, paper as gold, GOLD as paper
Or is the rule; lead pencil, paper and eraser?

But They're Gonna Get a Surprise

Oct. 08 08

They're gonna get a surprise
When she brings them to their knees
I asked God for no surprises
With a please
I'm begging God that I'll try's
To please Hymn on my knees
He said it's not Art's fault being no surprise
Art just likes to tease

Art thinks God is out of Her mind getting a prize
Of a lost person She sees
Loss of religions whys and lies
Religions where Jesus loves to see me
We talk it over tea
Also while eating pies
Religion gives us highs
Cause Jesus flies with me

People cries
With glee
Maybe someday we'll have back the bees
Maybe not having the fee to appease
The God that never dies

She is always bigger in size
Leaving me with sighs and whys
She try's us because of lies

Every Human has the Same Boss

The clergy say there is only one God.
So one God is our Boss.
Jews believe in one Supreme Being.
The Bible names Him as the Most High.
The Jews that seen God as Jesus,
converted themselves to Christianity.
These ex Jews were now persecuted Catholics.
Because the Jewish leaders hated Jesus,
more than Satan, they not wanting Jesus to fulfill the law.
People that knew everything wouldn't stoop as low as Jesus.
There is nothing worse than a Jew that hates God.
After seeing Him, except another Jew.
Catholic Christians started persecuting each other.
Different Catholics believed differently.
Some playing by rules as they pleased.
Like today the rules can change tomorrow unjustly.
They can get us coming and going.
Depending upon the direction.
Some religions are persecuted by their own religion.
because they believe their religion.
There is nothing worse than an ex Jew converted to Christianity
That is reconverted to be Jewish.
Because Christians do not believe the Bible.
They in reality are Jews not Christian.
I don't need a Mormon to tell me the Bible had mistakes.
The apostle Paul tells us Satan perverted some scriptures.
Mormons need someone to tell them of imperfections.

There is a difference between: prophet, profit and Prophet.
Some religions worship a prophet as a Prophet.
One is, one isn't God.
All religions are fighting against their other brothers.
Fighting because they are taught the same basic beliefs.
Be a Christian, do well and look out for number one.
No. it's be religious, repent and look behind your back.
Every human has the same Boss.
If we don't, people are wrong believing religion.

Fair Game

I am just a rookie bookie
Smoking a doobie eating a cookie
Tomorrow at noon we will take the loot
Out of the room, we being on foot

Soon our loot will be a boon
To some gloom and doom
They are the ones that look in books for money I took
The fools might as well look on the moon
Sweeping with a broom

The room is cool having a pool
Where some drool seeing boobs
I am on the stool near the pool
Smoking a Kool using my tool
I will soon be on the tube my name is Boog

Most old coots do not give a hoot about loot
I hide mine in a loose tooth, boot, booth
and under a hood when I could
at times there is a goof with a hoof on the roof
combing the wood testing my mood for good

Now people will have wood to cook food
From the bookies loot and tools
Some have stood with a spoon
Cooking good food with wood
From loot a rookie bookie took

Forgiveness

7/30/08

I tend to sin quite often.
Without any reason.
I try to bend the rules of ten.
Suiting my end.

Me bending the ten,
so as not to sin
Against Jesus my Friend.
until the end.

Jesus will mend my sin.
Knowing why, what and when
For Him to defend
Before the end.

Everywhere He's been
He's seen every sin.
Now He mostly grins,
At the Finns and at Yen.
Frowning at all Pen's
Where most drink, gin often.

Jesus will forgive my sin often.
©copyright 2008

Get Even

To get even
The world would have ended by evening
In America, Christians are not Christians
According to their Christian beliefs
So for God to end the world
Would be real Christian relief
From silly people who think they know the Bible

All so-called Christians are in trouble
Ask any nation if America made it double
The guys will blow bubbles or mumble
Then curse the people causing trouble

Anybody awake knows what's going on
Guess all people are asleep except this one
If people want right instead of might
Why don't the people in power do right?
Without the evil force of might?

People in power causes panic and fear
Read about the chronicles of American history
From year to year
Since 1800 America has only had one long depression
If disagreeing reread your history lesson
Because you've failed to recognize depression
Depression in this worlds daily conditions

Causes starvation worse than during Hoover's administration
Today one half of the world's population
Is dying of malnutrition
That's more than were alive during the thirties

Most do not live in the real world
They do not have time to recognize squirrels
Climb trees eat nuts and hide on the limb
When being hunted

In America, we each are the hunted

God is in Control

2009 Feb. 15

God is always in control of life.
God is always in control of death.
God is always in control of all His creation.

God can do everything.
Except assign an exact number on each angel head.
Or also to end His creation.

Then God could do nothing
When there is nothing to do.
After this world has ended.
Then that would be three things he Couldn't do.

That is if the world ended and He could not
Do anything about anything except nothing

But God also cannot die.
So that makes four things he can't do.
If God does die His creation would die with Him.
Thus, He could not have life continue.
The world would have ended upon His death.
Other words, if God dies there is not one thing
He can do except be dead.
Taking everything down with Him.

But that is two things He can do upon His death.
Meaning He does everything other than allow life.
Upon His death.
So He couldn't do anything about anything.
Nearly nothing at all.

Now go back to the four things above God can't do

God also can't be alive and permanently dead simultaneously
Jesus is always in control of the spirit world.

God Wants Her Money Back

2008 June 28

I now know,
how low,
I will have to go.
Crying foul dough.
Oh no! So much dough.
The Dow might as well be a hole.

I will go so low.
My pals, the gals: Jo, Chloe and Floe,
will bow to Joe, Lowell and Moe.

Wow God! You put me on a roll.
Making a mountain out of a mole hole.
After they stole the dough,
from your Dow and our cash flows.

A McDowel a Powell or a Coale
won't know,
what rolls under the coal.

Show the front row,
God's eyes glows and rolls,
of assets, others stole.

Show the front row:
Earthquakes rattles and rolls below.
With record flood flow,
Pole to Pole.

The accused vows, so much lower than zero.

Good or Evil

2009 Feb. 15

How can people be free?
In a world subjected to Satan?
Free to God is someone having a choice.
Between good and evil.
That's why evil came into the world.
For every ones freedom.

God gives people the choice,
Between good and evil
So they have a choice for themselves.

This evil world we live in is basically Satan's.
The Bible calls him the god of this evil world.
If this world is Satan's
I basically don't want to love this world.
Because it is evil.

Friendship with this world is enmity to God
Who Jesus is.
If we love this world we have less love for God.
Instead we have more love for Lucifer who god is.
Loving him for his evil ways to God.

People can be so cold
They will take your soul if you let them.

Did you sell out to Satan?

I Can't Draw a Picture

No tears in Heaven
For that worthless seventy seven
Most were church going not knowing of leaven
Now I really am unforgiven
For doing it on 7/17/97

Unforgiven is a term of reality during millennium
Anything I do now is forgiven
Cause I was the only one that knew Him at all

If people bawl
It's not because of what we did or saw
It's why they wanted this angel against the wall

Was it the Masons' or Shaws'
That wanted the Knackmus' to fall?
Just because they had control of the law?
For help, anyone of them could call
Receiving anything at all
Doing anything for me Pa and Ma
I can't draw
So don't ask for a picture of it all

If I Was 17 Again

Things would turn out exactly the same
Just change a few faces and places.
When a person is 47 years old
One looks back in life
Saying what if.
If only I would have done this
Or changed that.
I could have been rich.
Money never satisfies is a known fact.

What if I studied harder attending college?
I would probably ended up in a college gang.

What if I was real popular?
I then could have been another crooked politician elected to office.

What if I was preacher or teacher?
I would have misled a lot of students
With a verse for the worse

What if I lived on a Yellow Brick Road?
The road would still be bumpy with holes.

What if my parents were educated in Humanities?
Then we would be more part of an unjust system.

What if I was a lawyer?
I would have given and received a lot of kisses.

What if the farm was more productive?
Well, at least the deer and coyotes had more to eat.

If I was 17 having life's choices to do over again?
I think I would cry for grief.
If I knew then what I know now.

Lonely Me

Missed something in life
A girl, a friend, a mate for a wife
A prudent and true one to share good and strife
Now I have no one to say yes
I hope God will not love me less
I guess
He's the One who's really Cupid
Blessing one with a soul mate
So each will have someone to say yes
When it's time for bliss

This way a mate
Will not have to wait
For a serious date

So you won't have to fool around in town
Or in school to go down
Sometimes choosing when the prom gown
Goes down

Some guys don't know how to flirt
Girls will be hurt
She will call you a name lower than dirt
When the hand is placed up her shirt or skirt
Another will be hurt
She did not want more than to flirt

Drop the gown
Let's get down
On the ground
And fool around

Loner in Town

By Arthur R. Knackmus and Terry Kelsey 4/28/99

She looked so fine in her wedding gown,
As the train pulled out of this now lonely town.
I remember the day we looked at each other with a frown.
Now she is married to someone else and is leaving town.
We had many great dates if just cruising around town.
Oh, how sad I am she's going down to the other man's town.
Now I am a tearful ex clown, with my clown frown.
Praying she will come back to this now lonely town.
For another chance to see her smile at me so I could use this frown.
If only we could go out cruising around.

Oh baby, will you come back to town?
Oh baby, we could cruise around
We could go out tearing up the town.
Oh, if only you came back around.

Please girl shed that wedding gown.
God, I wish the train would bring her back to town.
Her beautiful eyes were brown.
Her cheerful mind was sound.
I always believed my eternal true love was found.
The girl would bring me up when luck was down.
Her true nature was of a queen, she should have a crown.
Just thinking of her smiles and touches makes my heart pound.
The sound will make me buy another round.

Oh baby, will you come back to town?
Oh baby, we could cruise up the town.
We could go out tearing up the town.
Oh, if only you came back around.

Many Indians in U.S.A.

When People are dealing with money,
Usually they deal as queer as a dollar bill.
Dollar bills are as queer as the ones dealing with them.

When selling ground some people don't care of right to might.
Basically it's might to right, any way to acquire this might.
Just any way to make little one's lives tight.

People want land now for money power and prestige.
Leading several queer millions into queer dowers.
People used to need land to make a living for their families.
Now some collect deeds and abstracts
To run smaller farmers out of business.

Helping small farms out of business leads bigger farms
To more land and those queer dollar bills.
Most land is stolen or borderline stolen.
This through land buyers lie's threats and deceptions.
Don't ask me how anybody can have a clear title to God's land.

The crooked ways of buyers and sellers leads to land monopolies.
This helps about all out.
Some helped out of business.
Others helped out into bigger business.
Being feared because of the queer dollar.

What the Christian farmers believe is right.
But they are wrong through their sinning actions of thefts.

Through the ages how many times has each acre been stolen in USA?

No Drink

12/17/08

Shawn shouldn't have been drinking
He should have been thinking
Instead of stinking drinking

He was to work on my kitchen sink
He, being in red ink
I guess I'm a ratfink

His elbow is now reddish pink
Cause he slipped in a dink
As he blinked
During his stinking drinking

Shawn thought he was in a skating rink
Holding his drinks
His feet slipped a link
Thinking he's Colonel Klink
While he's stinking drinking

At a blink of a wink
He almost fixed my sink
But he is now on Link and pink
In red ink
Still stinking drinking

Shawn should be thinking
NO DRINK

Not Fed

July 6, 2008

There was one year no one was fed.
God said, "He was fed up with the Federal dead."
Fed's, Ted and Ed were caught in bed before wed.
Getting and giving head while getting bred drinking a keg.
This happens in back of Ed's red shed.

God also dislikes the way Fed.'s dictated med's.
To the Med's Ed's and Ted's
God said of this, "My thinking head is bright red like it bled."
Why tread on the Red Skins who fled?
They also need bread and to be fed.

God said ", this year nobody gets fed."
I will keep all the bread in sheds.
I've read where people dread
this coming of the Lord's dead.
Many will die in bed,
For lack of bread.
The Fed.'s, invested in lead, instead of bread.
Fighting a crude oil war for gas heads.
Nobody told the Fed.'s not to tread on, God Heads'.

We are not going to be fed.
Also driving dreaded mopeds.
Because, of treading on God's head.

Not Less: But More Miserable

God gave me a miserable plight in life.
English words have so many different meanings.
Though they are spelled and pronounced exactly the same.
Sometimes the same word has opposite meanings.
I argue with others because I agree with them.
They, leaving mad because I was wrong.
Lots of times I am misunderstood by others.
Because my listeners cannot understand English.
Unless it is quitting time.

Some can be so cold, so can I.
How can I get along with people, when at times,
It is their lack of knowledge and my wrong name?
Some people do not have a vocabulary, only a memory.
Even, if they have a Master's degree.

If you disagree
Go ask a preacher or someone knowing.
The knowledge contained in Scriptures.
Is the best education of all.
This I have already proved.

Some with Masters Degrees do not believe in God.
Unless a member of the clergy.
They all live by faith.

Some cannot define (THE).
Usually it means the word following it.
Some are for education but it has to be done their way.
Even knowing they are wrong.
Education is the life of the people.
God said life is blood.
With this blood we live.

Pain is the result of sin in the world.
God will rid sin, through pain and suffering.
Then death.
Death is a painful transition back to the next life.
Life being eternal,
Till times end.
WHO KNOWS?

Poet of the Year

2008 July 8

In 2008 please make me a poet of the year.
Poet of the year is one title I would love to wear.
If I cannot wear it, tears will fall this year.
Washington D.C. doesn't need jeers, queers or tears to bear.
No jeers for ears to hear, causing tears.
This I could not bear.

It's clear, I am a poet to each person's eyes and ears.
I will get my clear writing mood in gear.
"Yes then," Next year Art will be poet of the year.

Nowhere does anyone come near, to this poet's ear.
Some poets drink beer or Everclear making some fear.
Their writing is unclear, then they swear.
Their poetry will never mirror mine.
Their poems will be nearer to unclear.
A fair pair of judges swears I may not be original that's clear.
Dear judges, I swear all my poems are original that's clear.
I, not a pair or more does these poems.
This honestly cause I fear for a bear in the air.

Dear Judges, I would love to be poet of the year!

She Will Take the Whole World Down

Oct 2008

Most of Iraqi and Kuwaiti gold
Was not sold
It was stole
Now the bullion is in American molds
Hope George is happily bold
Of getting stolen Iraqi gold

Hasn't anyone been told
God can also be cold and bold about gold

Over there in the Promise Land is also black gold
Of course America steals it by shiploads

The worlds and America's banks folds
Over the stolen golden bullion of gold
And especially over the stolen loads of black Gold

Is George gonna hold black and yellow gold?
Or is he gonna fold as told?
He'll just explode another load of bombs for gold
Next he'll recharge then reload
God wants Her gold back I'm told

I thought gold bricks were stored in California
But 25 truckloads were rolled into Nevada
Next on the list is Alaska and Canada
People only know bring flag from Florida
It must be good to be King of America

Shorts and Longs

If God bought and sold on the Board of Trade,
She would eventually go broke if She is honest.
Cause the Board isn't always long when it's short of products,
or short when the Board is long on products.
The object is to buy low sell high,
or sell high buying back low.
Lots of money people move the market,
in opposite directions it should follow.
Meaning its short when you're supposed to be long.
If there is a lot of a commodity you're supposed to play short,
when the market is really long, possessing much of the product.
Like I said before, you have to be long in a short market
and short in a long market.
That is if you want to make money.
God is Perfect so She can't sin even once.
She knows everything before it happens.
It happens She can't short a market when it is short of a product,
or have along position when the product is long.
There being an abundance of produce.
Because this is all wrong, being a sin,
She could never commit.
Thus God would end up on the wrong side of the Markets.
Being the honest person She is.

How can God invest in commodities when the markets are wrong?
Sometimes through lies and deceptions the Board is crooked.
Some people God doesn't want to Her Team.

Slaves to Satan

Some say I was lazy.
Art does not work for the money.
Being lazy
Lacking a honey
Me without money
They said I had

Some say they worked hard for money
I certainly agree with them
They, like me are slaves of Satan
I cannot disagree most worked hard
Some needing elbow grease from tipping a bottle

Lots of people help others out
Out of business using Satan's tactics
Working hard for him
Misled by others.
Free enterprise is a cutthroat society of fools
Businesses will help the others out
Running them secretly out of business
Some call them friend to face
Instead of keeping their end?

Why do people work so hard
Telling others how
Never knowing of the real world?
Lacking sense, while gaining cents
NEVER HAVING A CLUE

Takes One to Know One

1999

In life it's not what we know
Unless it's who we know and blow
I've heard many people say so
Saying nice guys suck, will put you in a 6 ft. hole
Unless you're a nice one to blow
That's the way the world works as a whole

Some at work get rug burn they're holes
Why do guys make girls sink so low
Guys say I wouldn't touch her with a 10 ft. pole
None of the girls could say no
Because they wanted part of the dough
Also craving after glow
From head to toe

Scratch mine I'll scratch yours just roll
I'll kiss yours, you bend over then bow
I'll bend over kiss mine now

It's the ultimate pleasure doing a gal

To get the dough
We've got to know
Who to blow
Knowing when to say no

The Best Days are Ahead of Us

Better days are ahead of us.
No, the best days are ahead of us.
So are the worst days.
We'll have wars that will make 1&2
Look like family reunions
Today more people are hungry in the world,
Than what were alive,
During the great depression.
I've got it figured out.
About every ten years,
There is a period of ten straight years
Of hard times and panics.
To know the future.
Look at the past
And read the Bible for understanding.
Some people don't know
The great depression is over.
Because their depressions
Have never ended.
God will have to intervene in due time.
Like He always does.
And make better days.
Remember, quick wealth isn't blessed.

The Blonde Bitch Next Door

2008

The blonde bitch next door
Is nothing but a little whore
All she wants from a man is to score
Against a wall a door
Or being parallel on the floor
Never getting enough, wanting more

The blonde bitch is always sore
Having many herpes scar sores
From her many scores
Having rug burned bodies from rugged floors.

I'll never screw another blonde bitch
She will give you head but also the itch
You'll scratch your itch hating the blonde bitch
Her snatch and crotch is a notch of a botch
Meaning she was no fair catch
Just a snitch of a bitch

There's one good thing about a blonde girl
She knows her tongue needs to swirl and twirl
Because that's what the guy's heads do during head
From the blonde bitch in bed

It's always been said
She's best at giving head in bed
Being unwed

She always swallows
Because her head is hollow
She won't even know me tomorrow
So she spreads her legs along with sorrow

Does anyone want to buy or borrow
The neighborhood blonde bitch tomorrow?

Bring plenty penicillin, quarters and protection.

Time Comes For Those Who Wait

These were the famous last words of a girl.
She's a make believe Witch loving a made up story'
Her times coming'
She said, "I will not marry my boyfriend."
"He has to wait."
TIME COMES FOR THOSE WHO WAIT

Her time has come and gone
Now she's out of time.
To the ones who are waiting.
Time must have come and gone.
The time and wait has gone to her head
'CAUSE TIME COMES FOR THOSE WHO WAIT

Waiting takes lot of time
But what comes after time
Some can't wait for
The ones holding in due time.
TIME COMES FOR THOSE WHO WAIT

When running out of time
Waiting for what comes
May not satisfy her
'cause her time has come and gone.
TIME COMES FOR THOSE WHO WAIT
SHE DIED

War is Life in Fast Motion

The Panama Canal during WW2
Was almost always open, letting ships through.
Because, Mexico needed passage exporting American crude
To the Germans Japs and other Axis war time crews.
Thus, they would then have a better chance winning WW2
This way Hitler gives to blondes with eyes of blue

When the Mexican American oil got through
American intelligence didn't have a clue
They done knew
Of unlawful Mexican crude
Passing through
Our rented slough

Mexico despised the few Jews
Also the Red White and Blue
This is not new to you

The Jews north of Mexico's crude
Were going to be placed in zoos.
Without stew
So the Mexican winners would have a better view
Of the losers who knew
They were the hated Red White and Blue

Mexico could produce more crude
Supplying both sides during WW2
All tank crews had fuel for the feud
Both sides intercepting crude

Leading American customs were Jews
Confiscating hot crude
Giving to Allied Jews and crews
For planes they flew

Someone blew the cue
Isn't war lewd rude and crude
War is: (LIFE IN FAST MOTION) a giant family feud
Dude, pay the devil his due

What a Great Man He Was

12/3/08

He was born in the United States of America.
Kings and Queens bow and play for him.
He's the most powerful human on earth.
This world was sort of built around Hymn.

For many years he was somewhat the music.
The movies and plays were of him, family and their enemies.
Royalties from books, songs, plays and movies should be his.
Every song I sing for this great one.

Books magazines and newspapers have many writings of him.
If he got paid his royalties he would be richest of all.
God has invented wireless telepathic puppets.
Yes, human has its own mind, ran by God.

God has shown me, humans don't know when to stop.
Stopping the wrong they are doing to the family.
God instilled in the wrong ones minds into thinking it's OK
(because) they go to Heaven, being Christian's through wrongdoing.

Art with Jesus made many millionaires and billionaires.
Art put West Salem high on Heavens maps.
Such as it's the capitol of Hell.
Heaven power was shown from West Salem through Hollywood.

Art was Gods' choice from the Big Bang beginning.
What's Art doing in a place like this?
He's playing a predestined man.
Wanna shake my hand?

What does it Matter?

2009 Feb. 16

I would just assume tobacco (nicotine) was an illegal drug.
Then Mary Jane was legal.
The population would begin to smuggle illegal tobacco.
While the legal Mary Jane would sit unsold on stores shelves.

The legal Mary Jane will sell cheap at stores in packs.
And tobacco will be sold by the gram or joint.
It being sold higher to dopers than Mary Jane is now.

More people will be arrested of fined then for illegal tobacco.
Use or possession than Mary Jane use now.
If the legal issues were switched.
It's all in people's heads of legal and illegal drugs.

It's usually an in crowd thing in the beginning.
Then turns into a habit or need.
Further on it's an addiction, sometimes chronic.

Tobacco is twice as addictive as cocaine
But they say tobacco is safer because it doesn't possess a drug
That is harmful enough to make it illegal
Like Mary Jane does.
Another reason tobacco is legal is too many are addicted
To it and smokers are voters at the polls.

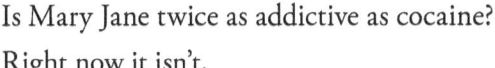

Is Mary Jane twice as addictive as cocaine?
Right now it isn't.
That's not to say companies wouldn't add inert ingredients.
Making Mary Jane much more addictive as tobacco is.

Any way if tobacco was illegal and pot legal.
Most smokers would still crave cigarettes rejecting legal pot.
Cigarettes would be a much higher priced commodity than pot.

Who Do We Send the Bill To?

1/22/09

It all started when Dale fell down on the Dail's trail.
Dale was drinking whale ale for his ills and ails.
He's now in a jail cell needing bail to get out of his Hell.
Dale doesn't even have a mill, can't pay bail.

The officer wanted to nail Dale on this trail.
After he failed the test walking a straight rail.
His trail test tailed off, he then had to urinate into a pail.
Well, Dale is pale because of drinking a pail of whale ale.
Pale of the Pell Mel system of Pall Mall.

Gail, the hailed arresting officer, confiscated stale beer
Near the dell.
He said ", I am going to tell the tale of Dale getting tail,
Near the shale pit and well.
We'll arrest any male that yells wails or sells ale,
To get female tail or her mail.

We'll send the male back to the Geihl flail chopper, ready to bale.
This, after bailing out from behind a Yale lock in a jail cell.

Someday Dale will marry Nell a female wearing a white veil.
Dale & Nell will be happy together sober. No Sale

Who Got Your Money?

Who thinks of tomorrow?
The one thinking, he takes everything to Heaven.
Instead of storing their future treasures in Heaven.
They save and store monetary treasures, here on earth.
This they think is their heavenly inheritance,
receiving from God what they made on earth.
Some people really do think they take, their
Greatest treasures with them, to heaven.
One can tell this, by the way a person leads his life.
God gives us everything we have.
He owns everything.
Sometimes He wants His possessions back.
In order to give them to someone else.
Whether they, being just or unjust.
We are only tenants of God's fortunes on earth.
Upon death we can't take the fortunes with us.
Unless our fortunes, were already stored, in heaven.

If Satan ends up with your money,
That's not all bad.
Cause what else is new in the world.
Satan gets a lot of money to work with.

Who is Responsible?

2008

Who is responsible for America's evil?
We Christian's know of Satan or the Devil.
Jesus allows the Devil's evil to exist.
Floods, earthquakes and tornadoes are vengeance from the Lord.
Drugs alcohol and tobacco are for Satan's use.
Poverty, illiteracy and illegitimacy are from unbelief in God.
Farmers and the whole food chain poison the produce.
Obesity, deformities and ills such as cancer are from additives.
The water is also unfit to drink causing sickness.
Crazy people in physco wards are from how they were treated.
Gangs in the country and cities are made and caused by people.
Evil done to us by the ones mentioned here are worldly.
Are people responsible for wars and evils they bring?
Do we blame the devil and his angels for our evil?
Do we blame Jesus and His angels for America's evil?
Blaming Jesus because evil will exist till He returns.

Jesus makes us who we are
*who is to blame for what they do?

We are still responsible for what we do
*though we can't help it who we are.

Who is to blame for wrong in America? OURSELVES

Who Says So?

Human was not the first life on earth.
Chaos preceded human life.
Angels preceding before chaos.
God has been alive forever
His world's end is never
This world's end is nearer
Who knows?

The angels rebellion brought war to Heaven
Earth ended in chaos
Lucifer and his angels were thrown out
Man replaced, these fallen angels

Man's existence
Brought God's death and resurrection
God was the second Adam as Jesus
The patient man on the cross was God

If perfection did not die on the cross
Who did and why?
Some say one did die, a fake
Atom can settle this at will
It was here first
Atoms have squatter's rights
In this world it is the worst fear of the two

Some want to start over from square one
Destroying one, then create a new universe
The heat is on

Who Won?

2007

Blonde Wonn, won one, on John Wand
Mr. John, won one, on Wonn Wand.
No one, gets one over, on John Wand, who won.
Unless it's Ron Wand or Shawn Wonn.
Ron Wand, won one, for Wonn Wand
Who's against, Blonde John Wand
Ron Wonn, won one against cousin Don Juan.
Don, toughest of the Juan's and Wand's.
Ron Wand's three blonde sons; Wonn John and Ron Jr.
Are done gone.
Leaving Ron Wand, against Don Juan
Don Juan, his sister Dawn Juan and cousin
Juan Wand, won.
These three vie for number one
Not Ron Wand or blonde Wonn.
Dawn Juan and Ron lost, due to notoriety.
Don Juan, won for the Juan's, Wand's, and Wonn's.

Words to Me

March 21, 2008

Quick to change ones, mind.
Slow to take action.
Menacing enough to be irritated.
Frightful in a way, leading to fear.
Scorned, torn apart.
Sexy made for early withdrawal.
Anxious before having, anxiety.
Restrained by religious means.
Brought down lower than dirt.
Trusted till busted, bankrupt.
Unlawfully prosecuted through legal ways.
Revered because of knowledge.
Properly educated through proper reasoning.
A beginning, with no end.
Evil to the point, of no return.
Reasoning without doubt.
Power to no limit.
An end with no beginning.
Make believe life of unseen world.
Objecting decisions with brief hesitations.
Seeing the unseen.
Hearing the unheard of.
Feeling the unfelt having no pattern.

Am I?

12/25/09

What if you are the devil
And know it?
Are you going to turn from rejecting God's authority
Requesting God to still give your angels that fell
A freedom of choice between good and evil
Or are you going to obey God.
Helping Jesus ridding this world of sin
That you have brought upon yourselves and others?
Is it really better to rule in hell
Than to serve in heaven
That a lot of people down here believe?

Satan, God will not forgive you
For doing what everybody else would have done
If they were in your shoes at that time
Because you like me are just puppets of God
People want a choice not liking
What to do or request forced to one choice
In God's government
Now all we humans are hell-deserving sinners at best
But can receive salvation from God
Humans are only on earth because God kicked
One third of the angels out of heaven to earth
Humans replaced the Fallen Angels on

Why are people so mad at the devil?
Blaming him because he is the main reason we're here

Satan hates us humans because;
God offered each human salvation free grace & atonement
While the fallen ones are down there
Locked up in chains forever

The devil is not going to change his ways
Unless God who Jesus is allows him to change

Fallen Angel's Second Chances

2009

When we humans die
Going to hell as our eternal reward
We'll always ask Jehovah
For a second chance

What if this world is our second chance?
What if we people are Fallen Angles?
This being, our last chance for salvation.
A chance people never think of.

We people on earth,
Live in a place worse than hell
Hell is defined as; Eternal separation from God

Yahweh must be through some day
Giving second chances
To people who are out of time and place

Will Jesus end this universe someday?
Creating another later?
To give more chances
Until the Fallen Angels
Changes their minds?

How long does it take for a fallen one to realize
They have been sent to hell on earth
If nobody tells them so?

We people on earth are separated from God
But not necessarily eternally.
Unless we follow Satan instead of Jesus
Fallen Angels have no grace or salvation from God
In turn they will do anything to hurt God

I Found the Devil

Aug. 8, 2009

I found the devil.
He's in the Churches.
He's in the schools.
He's at country fairs.
He's never fair. BEWARE!

I found the devil.
He's in each home.
He's around when each is alone.
He's always around and he roams.
He's the Prince of the Power of the Air.
He's never fair. BEWARE!

I found the devil.
He's in the Bible.
He's also in our other books.
He's in the government.
He lacks atonement.
He's a liar.
He's never fair. BEWARE.

Money Thang

12/25/09

In America it's a money thing
It will take all the dollars men can bring
For only a one night fling
Before or after the State's sting

If the cop's sting
Was before the fling
You'll need a quarter to ring
Somebody that won't sing
About your wrongs of a G string
Saying only you have wings
Never would hurt a thing
Missing the one thang
A one-night fling

America is a circus ring
People trying to avoid police strings

Many swing for a fling
Some in a corrupt ring
This a band of thugs to steal things
Their lips are tied never to sing
Receiving their pay from the corrupt ring
Some of their pay went to the cop's sting
So the thugs could continue the ring
Giving the money to cops for them to swing
Doing a one night thang
They also sworn not to sing
Of their own corrupt ring

People do not know its money that makes the world go round and round

Strange

8/10/09

God can be a little strange
Strange to we humans, in good ways.
He can make the lowly.
Come into power.
Or bring down the higher ups
On the society ladder.
Making them fall so low.
Instead of leading they follow.

God can make the lowliest one.
In a civilization, to become King.
Or have little and small.
Defeat big and tall.

God has many ongoing projects.
Most humans don't see these.
Many times His projects.
Are not detected.
Because we fail seeing His strange ways.
Affecting our strange lives.

Teach a Peach

8/23/09

Schools can teach
Freedom of speech
But can't teach
When they do impeach
It's because of one's speech

Schools can't teach
Life's a beach
When each
Is a leach
A leach for each peach

Schools can't teach
Each peach we reach
Has no leach
Except the one that reaches
Picking the peach

If smart one's believes freedom of speech
They will be impeached
If they practice what they preach
Being fired to teach

Life's really a beach

Poor Friend Shawn

3/1/09

I have a good friend named Shawn.
His assets and money are all but gone.
This Shawn has a heart of gold.
He will do anything for anyone, I'm told.

To get money
he has to scrap out.
He's so strong and stout
lacking a loving honey.

He is really friendly being good-natured.
In my book of who's who he's featured
As one of my best friends ever.
Because he would give me his last dollar.
If I am hungry he will feed me quail.
He always talks well of my family, especially Dale.
Shawn's health isn't very well
Cause his ankle hurts and swells
He is continually in pain.
This pain almost drives him insane.
He must walk with a wooden cane.
Taking medication potent as Novocain
To kill the constant throbbing pain.

Shawn just wants to be friends with most.
If someone isn't his friend
They would probably backstab the Holy Ghost
Stealing from the one who was played friend.
His family tree
Is partially Cherokee
He believes in Christianity.
Believing Jesus is God Almighty

When selling wood he believes in delivering a full measure.
He will not cheat customers, because of his heart, his treasure.
Maybe someday he'll find a woman for pleasure.
He would never cheat on her during times of leisure.
Shawn treasures the simple things in life.
Like family, friends and a wife.
This is plain, life is always strife.

The story of his life is he has always been without.
Without a lot of cash for extras, no doubt
But possessing a heart of gold,
that can't be bought nor sold.

Easy for You to Say

2006

If someone has done you wrong
No matter how long
We are repeatedly required to forgive
The wrong doer of evil
That is being a true forgiven Christian

It's easy to say this
But the practice is difficult
And in some places and cases rare

It takes a true forgiver
To be a forgiven Christian

It's easy to say forgive
To do it is difficult
Especially if the wrong doing continues
For a long long time

At times it's easy for me to forgive wrong
Other times I like God,
Don't forgive until time heals wounds

The problem is not with me forgiving
It is whether Lord Jesus is forgiving

That's easy for me to say
Because I know where I am going for eternity

Every Knee Shall Bow to Me

Jan. 21, 2010

God says someday every knee shall bow to Him.
Whether in hell, on earth or in heaven above.

About 2000 years ago God lived in Jerusalem.
There they know of, hearing about Jesus' love.

All Jews will eventually kneel to Jesus.
The true Jews are spread over all nations.

Muslims will all kneel to Jesus.
Who do you think Allah is?
Yes, He's Jesus.

The Pope and his Catholics will kneel.
So will religions worshipping cows.
Every one kneels and bows,
But how now?

I don't know about the Dow.
But all the investors will kneel and bow.
Someone is here greater than THOU.
Some use hankies some towels.

There comes a day when everybody
Knows there is a God.
Especially the worldly and ungodly.

Jehovah's' Witnesses will kneel to Jesus.
Listen to J.Ws. squeal to Jesus.
Yes Jehovah is a Wheel, being Jesus.

Satanist wants to deal with Jesus
Jesus says your gods are Satanic Lucifer's.
You've dealt with him for earthly power.
You've knelt with him for earthly dowers.
Your hearts will melt for Jesus' Heavenly power.

Satanist skinned people alive for human pelts.
How can Jesus forgive what dying felt?
The burning welts from belts.

Mormons believe they have a perfect religion.
Michael, bring in another legion.
Being angels sent to Salt Lake region.
Conquering the Mormons perfect religion

Jesus will conquer the heathen
None will be left breathin.
While all are kneeling.
Here on earth in hell and heaven.

Who will be the Brethren?

Gangster

Feb/7/2010

People have always told me
They are in the mob,
Or know someone close in the mob.
They say they can screw me up somehow.

Yes, they use power threats.
Getting what they want and request.
Simultaneously calling me friend to face.
Plotting secretly to stiff me hard in the end.
If only over a six-pack of beer or a $200 car.

What is this organized mob?
Bader than a lynch mob or being rustled.
I think I have found them by accident.
It's a brotherhood of an association of brothers.

I can't tell you how I found them.
If I did tell all
I would have to kill you
The Associations rules, ruling America.
For that matter the whole world.
This Association has nothing to do with the
Singing rock group The Association.

Someday my family
Will own corporate association of Thy Brotherhood.
I want to save them!

Why save them?
If their boat sinks
Me being the Captain,
Goes down with the ship.

Am I a victim of my own corporate problem?

Me being an associate in the association of The Association.
Will not associate myself with foolish friends any more.
For if you know anymore,
I would have to kill you.

Not really cause", GOD TOLD ME!"

God Disciplines

Jan. 27, 2010

It's now year 2010 A.D.
God is disciplining America with the whole world.
Because majority doesn't know
Who is God!

God is Jesus Christ!
Called King of the Jews.
Jesus also is the Christian God.
Most Christians do not accept this.

I hope Jesus doesn't discipline the world
Like He did unto us!
Isn't there an easier way?
For Jesus to tell of His Kingdom?

Do people realize most of America
Reject Jesus' teachings?
Mainly of Him being God.
Most of the world religions reject Jesus.
Following false gods or prophets.

In America Jesus as God is a minority.
This leaves the majority as non-believers
Them to me playing ATHIEST lives.
Why have public prayer in schools.
When most of prayers are against believers?

If people knew they're wrong
Why would they blame God for world's catastrophes
and destructions aiding few people.
Benefiting few people.

Jesus shows His reining power.
He's shown it before
He'll do it again
An unbeliever saddens God greatly.

Most don't care after told!

History Speaks

Jan. 24, 2010

What a dark era for the world!
The world is losing God's love.
Falling to lower god's love.
Falling to love of money, lust and fornication.

World is losing His love of Him.

More persons love Satan
God Jesus isn't going to love those persons.
People do not know what they are doing.
This includes me.

I say, "Do as thou shall see fit."

I don't know if I'm helping Lord Jesus.
People doubts of my writings.
Doubting I put together words and sentences.
Believing to them Arts a fake, for trouble.

Cursed be the ground you stand on!

I pray for Jesus to come back.
This way he can increase His friends.
Not destroying His enemies.
He will turn them to friends.

The meek shall inherit Heaven.

God may not love anyone in this world.
If God ends His love for us.
People are losing their love for God.
They don't understand history

Or His tory!

Last Poem

Jan. 22, 2010

This will be the last poem
I will ever write for you

Did God create a mistake?
That couldn't be corrected?

He wants to build His world around me.
Boy, are they in for a big surprise!

Do we all want God's vengeance
Directed upon America that we sorely need?

Jesus can make armies have enough friendly fire.
To totally destroy their own selves.
Soldiers wouldn't even have enough sense to know.

God bring up Gideon and his selected army.
Do you want the world's army's to do?
To America what was done to us?
Or is Jesus supposed to forget about everything?

Is this a breach against God if all is forgotten?
Not carrying out the book of Revelation?
What about all the others throughout time?

Forgetting will take a long long time.

Time will tell.
A hundred life times to wear it down.
See ya in hell.
Destroyer Angel, Angel of Death, Angel of mercy.

God just forget about it.
They don't even know what they did or are doing.

Too late for states fate
NO FAIR
Building my world around you.

Mission Control We Have a Problem

January 19, 2010

We're going have a beautiful Word and world.
But when Jesus when? When?
Win win God please when.

Are we supposed to wait forever?
Getting our money back.
So they can steal it again?

Jesus is giving me the world.
What then does it matter to me?
Of the pain, money or what each sacrificed?

As the martyrs throughout history
If Gods forgetting them is a breach of God.

C.J.L said animosity to neighbors is the worst sin.
Dad said respect of persons is the worst sin.
I say blasphemy to God is the worst sin.
Because this Blasphemy is not forgiven.

Respect is what God wants.
To Him, not others.

Why do rockets blow up, Mission Control?
This God's way of getting attention.

It's not only we who rocks the boats.
But some who quotes

We can't buy God's love with money.
We need love, repentance, forgiveness a honey.

Is God going to breach space?

Prove It

1/20/10

My faith and beliefs
Are of Christian and Jewish natures
To me One Supreme Being is God Creator
He's also called the Most High, Jesus, Yahweh,
Jehovah and hundreds of other names as such.

I know there is a higher source of power.
Through my Christian nature it's our Jesus with His angel's
Controlling this world of sin and false beliefs.
They allow this to happen
Some times through false prophets

Jesus is King of the Jews.
He a Prophet spelled with a capital P for God.

I can't be 100% sure Jesus is God Creator
If I was 100% sure of Jesus as God,
I would know instead of believe.

Jesus leaves a doubt in all minds,
Including mine of being 100% sure of His true existence.

I am 100% sure of another power.
It's not human
It has to be God.
But I can't PROVE IT.
That is of His existence.
The reason is my less than 100% knowing Jesus is God.
God showed me 100% He is here, being real.
GOD PROVED IT.

I have a 100% faith as Jesus is God.
Though not 100% belief or sure of Jesus.

How can someone be 100% sure of God
And not be called know it all?
Instead of a believer

Even though the believer has less than 100% faith.
Then he still couldn't be know it all.

-If there is someone who knows 100% certainty,
of Jesus a God
It could be PROVED and that someone could PROVE it.

This someone wouldn't have any faith
In God's existence.
Because He would be 100% sure.
Lacking faith

Still after knowing 100% certainty of God
We would lack faith.
Knowing there is a God.

When people cannot acknowledge His wondrous works.
He, God letting the devil blind human minds.
Would this be true faith if one believes?
Though not seeing His projects or works?

When God quits showing His works,
Just like in Biblical times.
People will quit believing in God.
Needing the faith we sorely need
When God showed the Egyptians He was God
The Egyptians would not bow to Him after knowing.
Yet the Israelites knew also.
In due time Jews forget going to the wayside.
After God had showed for certain whom He was.
Jesus PROVED
Yet people still go to Satan
Satan knows the scriptures well.

Is knowing also faith?
Or is knowing classified as one having
Little or no faith at all?

It's better to believe and never seen.
Than to have seen and know.

I can't be 100% certain of Jesus as God
But I can be 99.9% sure.
This makes me a man of little faith.
Knowing 99.9%

Though I have little faith
I dearly believe Jesus loves me as much
Or more than anyone.
This because I know
But can't be 100% certain of Hymn.

So a man of little faith

Can humbly and peaceably die knowing Jesus.

Do people see verses and Bible doctrine

Can have opposite meanings at times?
PROVE it
I can't
Cause I don't have 100% proof
But do have proof beyond a reasonable doubt
That is the law in America

If Jesus is here on earth.
He could not PROVE it
No matter what He PROVED, disapproved. Approved
Unproved, reproved, moved or loved.

PROVE IT

Shoot Me, Drug Me, Burn Me and Bury

Jan. 22, 2010

Based on a true story.

Welcome to Little Egypt
Drug capitol of America

Let's have a house burning
No I meant to say to Rick
"Let's burn one."

Call one of our buddies
You mean another copper, lawyer
Or some nark snitch druggies?
To get Mark, Leo or O'Bob tomorrow?
What about Sheriff's morals to Orels?

Even the Wise men, Williams or Bangdeer theory
Is people's opinion of Heavens story

Satan and Lonny own Vaseline
Partially their glory
U all will roll in it is Heaven's greasy story.

Snider sells, Williams tells.
William Tell would be proud to tell
Of pictures Williams tried to sell.

Wells tells us who Robin Hood is
He's the one with laced legal drugs enhancing mood.
Coopers, robbers and lawyers all the sellers
They a bunch or liars.

Here, cops don't want young persons in Pool Halls.
Cause they won't spend as much money on drugs.
To get arrested with.

Meaning less income for their system
Of unjust justice.
Thus, keeping the system working at Court House.
The Police State of cops, States Attorney's, the law
Had drug money to burn.
From pay offs and kick backs
Of little criminal cliques
Here in Little Egypt.
A place of corruption
No better than Eqypt

Of course power of the pen
Is mightier than the sword.
Depending what penitentiary
Spoken of or referred to

West Salem may be capitol of hell

Welcome to drug capitol of world.
Edwards Country also a killer's paradise

Jesus wept
In Little Egypt
As killed in paradise swept
While the sleeping Giant slept.
Sending others to Hell's crypts

Jesus weeps
We were asleep
Their souls for Satan to keep

Bury the story theory
In minds of guilty

Satan wins your souls for eternity

Turn the Other Cheek

1/21/2010

The Bible says to turn the other cheek.
How many times is a person supposed to turn?
Which cheeks is God referring to?
Are people to get blistered cheeks?
Having sore jaws and cracks.

I don't think they would spit on my cheeks,
If the cheeks were burning being on fire.

Are people supposed to get sore cracks?
Cracking the sores during life?

I do not think God meant for Christian
To be an enemy to another Christian.
Unless they cause the other to sin.

Do people want firing squads for juries?
This could be arranged.
For better or worse

Figuratively we've had the sore butts.
Squeaky wheels usually get greased first.
Some frequently, some permanently.
Don't grease the Wheels in the Sky.

Does anybody else get tired of turning?
Above and or below?

Turned the other cheek.
This done to no avail
When are the Wheels in the Sky arriving?

Tell them to turn.

What is it Worth?

Feb. 5, 2010

What is it worth for U.S.A. to get completely out of debt?
Soon United States will be 15 trillion dollars in red ink.
This is just the Federal debt.
Not counting each state's debt local debt and individual debt.

I think we need to pick a State here in U.S.A. sell it to China.

If inflation does not continue,
Making inflation turn to deflation
Our debts could double over night,
If we are lucky.
This not even assuming the interest rate increases.

If interest rates go up to 50% on our worth more money.
Our dollar bills won't be worth less any more.

Why are people against worth more money
Instead of possessing worthless money
People now possess?

If interest rates go to 50%, our national payments
For 30 years would increase 300 times
If we never borrow another dime.
It would be twice as hard again
A total of 50% not each year. Only for one year
Staying there for the duration of 30-year loans.

According to my figures if they are all across the board.
If would be 600 times harder to pay back 15 trillion dollars
If given 30 years to do so.
With 50% interest and 50% deflation for one year.
At today's dollar it would be; 9,000 1,000,000,000,000 $ bills
Of federal debt in 30 years, this if no more was borrowed.
I will write it also.
Nine thousand, one trillion dollar bills.

Do people see why our government
Wants money to be worth less
Instead of worth more?

Would a worth more dollar
Make a dollar worthless?
Making the value of the dollar
On markets go up or down?

If interest rates rise to 50% with the 50% deflation for one year.
Would the value of the dollar have a tendency to rise or fall?
Or would it even matter by this time.
I don't think it would make any difference
Cause China would have all the money and income.
If China has the dollars they are the ones who
Have the most to gain. That is JUST PLAIN FREE RULES
OF FREE ENTERPRISE
If America defaults on her loans
CHINA WOULD THEN DEMAND LAND
That is nothing but fair according to our fair laws in U.S.A.

I still say sellem Illinois or at least Chicago.

China also has the most to lose having the money.
China probably would not want Chicago.
They might want Little Egypt, which is South of Chicago.

When the value of the dollar goes up 50% along with 50%
Interest rates and the one-year of 50% deflation
Our debt in dollars for a 30-year loan would be:
(18,000)(One trillion dollar bills)

Where are the gasoline and or Vaseline?
And who are going to have sore butts?

I say, "Let's sell China a lifetime dower to Illinois."

Use Federal and States power of Eminent Domain.
That's how Israel got its land to make a country.

Why can't USA condemn all Illinois land if it were to save
What's left of a Right Union?
How many times in the past has U.S.A. condemned land?
For purposes as such?

Yes, they have done it in the past and will do it again.
I think we need to avoid war with China.
Not at all cost but at their cost?

China doesn't want United States money
China just wants our lands
When is the CALL date?
America cannot get out of debt.
Unless we default. (CANCEL)
Sell something or be given something.
(THE WORLD WAITS, call date)

Personal Poet of God

As I look up to the sky
I ask why?
Isn't my brain fly?

I try
Not to lie
While I cry
Till tears dry

Jesus upon High
Please let me fly
Understanding why
Some things can fly
Or Knowing why
All species die

Jesus, you are the Eye in the Sky
Watching as we slowly die

My grandfathers used a scythe
To tirelessly cut wheat or rye
They also needing to be fly

Jesus, to You, I will always say hi
Never saying good bye
I pray God, please make me fly

Hole in His Head

2010

Why did Lance get a hole?
Shot in his head?
Ask me, King Arthur
I will tell you.

Lance was a drug dealer.
And yet worse, a thief and a liar.

Why wouldn't Lance,
Just give me back my impact wrench?
I don't know why not,
But if you ask Bucky Junior
We could get the answer.

To me,
Lance got what he deserved.
"A bullet hole in his head"
The only thing I regret
Is that more people including some of his relatives
Did not receive their deserved
Hole in the head also.
Getting the vengeance from God
Those people deservedly deserved.

Why Believe?

April 20, 2010

People actually believe the Pledge of Allegiance.
It states, "I quote."
Liberty and Justice for all.

Did or do all veterans receive justice.
You can try to tell me there is justice in America
But a person has to die to get real justice from God.

The justice I am talking about
Is true justice from Jesus
We each receive when we die.
Not the so-called fake justice the American way.

What about Liberty for all?
Do you know, one million women are forcibly
Locked up in America forced to give sex?
And over 50,000 children are sacrificed to the devil
Every year in America?
Is this Liberty and Justice for all?

People do not want to hear all the truths about America.
Is the Constitution to be believed?
All it is, is a piece of paper with words.
People decides what justice is
People are far from perfect.
All we imperfect persons are nothing
But a herd of Hell deserving sinners.

Hell deserving sinners invented the Constitution.
Where is the Liberty and Justice for all?
What I am saying is that some of us are
Left out of justice being scapegoats.
God is making a mockery out of the USA.

A Free Country?

April 20, 2010

America started out free
Free from freedom that is.
Here in the free America slavery was freedom.
According to our laws of freedom.
Of the Constitution.

Stealing the Indians land for free
And putting slaves to work
Gave freedom its biggest start.

The Indians were free to
Buy back their own land,
They freely roamed on.
This was they could freely buy back freedom.
They done had before presidents.

Americans have absolutely no remorse.
From stealing their free country.
So idiots like me can freely write.
About freedoms that do not exist.

Women could not vote
Because they were considered property,
In this free country
Of men not women.

Why do Christian Americans believe we are free?
When Satan is the god of this evil world?
We Americans are subjects of Satan.
Just like the rest of the world.
We Americans are not really free, by any means.

All Men Are Not Equal

4/22/2010

God created all men equal
But in life's end are not equal

People have an equal right to,
Accept or reject Jesus and His Teachings.

People die then plead with God
They did not have a chance to know Hymn

Maybe the accused Jesus is wrong
Not giving each person an equal chance
To accept Hymn as God.

People claim to be Christian
But do not believe in the Christian God
Who Jesus is

How can those so-called Christians get to the Paradise?
Jesus speaks of, upon ones death?

Persons in America have equal chances
According to the Constitution
To believe in their own God

But if they don't believe in Jesus
They can't be equal
Unless they all are enjoying themselves in Hell.
With all the other equals
That disbelieved in God

All the disbelievers are equally unhappy in Hell
Where they equally belong.

Too many Bosses were the cause of inequality.

Inequality also exists in Heaven
But there they are equally happy, being content
With the inequality that exists in Jesus's Kingdom.

Not Shy

April 22, 2010

God is not shy with me.
About Heaven and Hell throughout eternity.

People absolutely do not care of God.
If they do
Why is there so much vengeance?
In this world
Where everybody says they know God
And are a bunch of great Christians
Of good nature.

If people know God
Where is the forgiving and forgetting?

People who are Christians or some what
Claim to be Christian.
Are lost causes in Gods world.
Cause they cannot see Him
Or His ways in this evil world.

God disciplines the ones whom He loves.
This I know is true.
Cause I know
God loves me more than Life itself?

Why don't Christians wake up?
Finding God in this world of evil?

A worshiper listens to the preacher preach.
Then goes home
To continue doing what he always has done.
Doing to others what he thinks is right.
Being right to God in his human eyes.
But not necessarily right in God's eyes.

Just because a Christian thinks he is right.
Doesn't make him right to God!

God is not shy. Speaks fluently and is always right!

Lottery

April 22, 2010

How can persons be so greedy?
Spending money on a State controlled lottery.
A lottery meant to steal money from corrupt education.

The educational system may never receive
Or not receive much of the money.

All the lottery is
Is a legal tax
Cause that is where the money goes
TAXES!

If someone wins
They pay taxes on it
So in realty they don't win all the money
Much of it is paid in TAXES.

So the lottery is a tax
On gamblers to win money
These are the losers against paying TAXES.

People are against paying TAXES
So why do they play a corrupt lottery?
When playing, all they will ever do is pay TAXES
Whether they win or lose.

Either way, they eagerly, happily agree to pay TAXES
Paying to keep a system of corruption afloat.
Even though they 100% disagree with it?
The TAXES

Imagine That

April 22, 2010

I was once thinking there was no God.
Just death and darkness in the grave.
Upon ones succumbing on earth

If Jesus, who is God
Doesn't exist or ever did exist
Then we are just dead
Like the devil worshipers say.
Laying there in total darkness
In our grave, which is eternal

Imagine there is a God
And Heaven and hell truly exists

Some people still lay in darkness
Because they rejected Gods' ways of justice.
Vengeance is the Lords.

Lots of people are dead living in the darkness of Hell
Heaven is a house of many Rooms
How many rooms are cold, empty with no light?

Many people are living the After Life
In dark empty rooms filled with grief

Imagine that

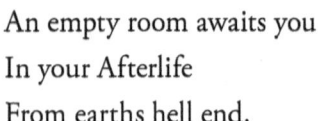

An empty room awaits you
In your Afterlife
From earths hell end.

Some people just do not get it!!!
There will always be an empty room waiting for you!!!

Have you got just even a prayer of a chance???
IMAGINE that!!??

Print Truths!!!

Aril 22, 2010

All I do is write truths
To best of my abilities
What's wrong with that?

Sometimes I get carried away
Writing too much of the truth
That's better left unsaid.

To tell the truth
If people are told the truth
Then the truth is more than they can bear
Cause the truth is what hurts
More than a pack of lies of truths

If the truth hurts
Then I have hurt a lot of others
With my truths

To tell the truth
Nobody, by now cares about the truth

Too many people from truths
Have been hurt from telling the truth
This includes me

Truthfully God chose me
To tell the truth
Cause no one else would

Tell the truth
Cause the truth hurts

Who is crying for the truth?
Yes it's all true
Say it, write it, and publish it!!??
The plain truth

Up and Down Limits

There is nothing hard about simple math.

If daily trading limits are 30 cents.
In each direction
Why is it so hard to figure out?
They get you coming and a going?

You can lose or make 60 cents
Per bushed
In one trading day?

30 cents up
30 cents down
Equals a possibility of 60 cents
If you buy and sell
On the high and low of the day.
Of these markets.

Do my figures lie?
Or am I a figure that is a liar?
Or a liar that figures?

America Chose the Wrong Side

2010

Why didn't America choose the side of Germany in WW1?
Because they did not want to. That is why!

Was Germany all wrong?
For blowing up so-called neutral American ships?
Those ships hauled bullets and bombs and what ever
To Germanys enemies
That was also American enemies.
But that is free enterprise
Nobody tells us what to do
Or how our families are supported
America will get rich any way She wants

If America is neutral then stay neutral
And keep America bombs and bullets at Home.
Because all you will do is start another war
When this one is over.
Nothing will be settled
Only another war to fight

Nobody pays any attention to the history lesson!!!

America was really on Germany's side in the first war.
Until it came time to enter the war.

In the end ever country got screwed
Except America that had a lot of heroes

America eventually got screwed with another one of her
DEPRESSIONS
Germany defaulted on the loans from America
Sending ALL the worlds governments to DEPRESSIONS
Why did God, who Jesus is, allow this depression?

God did this to teach the world lessons
But they don't teach lessons in school
Only reading writing math and history
Nobody is taught true lessons in school
School in America is generic

Nobody is 100% right in war.
Regardless what is taught in school

America is wrong at times
It is all a money trip
Called free enterprise

Try telling so called winners turned to losers
God sent a dictator
But people still do not listen to God

They then only pray and want during WW2
Caused by WW1 the war called to end all wars

How can a Christian nation be so stupid of life?
There will always be war until Jesus comes back
War started in Heaven

And Heaven would have been destroyed
If God had not stopped His angelic puppets.

People don't listen or care about God
There are Chaplains in the military
Why don't they preach the truth of God?
To the presidents?

Preachers are afraid in the military
Never holding up for right
Because they know they will be shot for right
Preachers just will not preach the Bible
Out of mainly fear and ignorance

Nobody wants to listen
Only tell others what to do

I am a nobody and I listen and tell others
Of life's imperfections
But it is not too late for God's judgments
Of our government

If people do not fight for God
They are killing for all the wrong reasons

Do people still want to argue?
Why doesn't America pick on someone with an atomic bomb?

Our mistakes through time
Is what we are left with today and throughout history?
Armageddon will make 1&2
Look like family reunions

To what is to come in the end.

How many times has a veteran said
If I knew then
What I know now
I never would have gone?

One woman had 13 brothers in WW2
She said when they all came home
For their family reunions
All 13 agreed
Back in 1945
America should have tested the atomic bomb
On Albion Illinois
I don't know why

Maybe that would have ended all wars?????????????????????????????????

Unforgiven

April 24, 2010

Unforgiven is not even a word
But is used by us often

People seldom forgive
Some one that did some wrong

The unforgiving people
Might have well done the wrong
The unforigven wrong doer did

This is according to Gods laws

If we do not forgive the wrong
Done to us or by us
Then God won't forgive the person
That is unforgiving
Meaning the unforgiving people are also unforgiven
By God who is forgiving

Is this Gods way of being unforgiving?

If the unforgiving people are unforgiven by God
Are these unforgiving people guilty of the crime?
They are unforgiving to?
Even though they did no wrong
Except to be unforgiving?

People unforgiving are as wrong as their unforgiven
The unforgiving being unforgiven
By our forgiving God

Who says unforgiving is unforgiven to Hymn
Thus UNFORGIVING is UNFORGIVEN!!!???

Build World Around Me

4/25/2010

Jesus and Satan want to build their worlds around me.
Me, being simple and stupid
Shows Jesus did not have many choices
To choose from.
I am just a Kiss on His List.

Jesus has secrets
So does Satan
I don't care of secrets.
Why can't I tell the facts of this world?

To this world
Maybe I am a little crazy.
I forget, delete, debate and lie with reasoning.
Insisting God forgive me.
I knowingly work for Hymn
With Satan staring directly at me
Or vice versa

No one is perfect but me
I Arthur is the perfect specimen
For God and Satan to deal with
Because no one would have suspected
This from the Beginning

When I turn cut the lights at night
I like others never know what tomorrow brings
Though I do know what to expect
Whether it is good or bad.

God and Satan building their tomorrows
Around me, unto their satisfaction

I am the songs, tunes and music.
I will be the new movie and old movie
I will be the new news and old news.
Even though this is worldly
I am putting up my treasures in HEAVEN.

Who gets the best of all possible Worlds?
I do of course
Except for the insane part
Maybe the world is going insane.

Well, that's me!
What will be will be?
Tomorrow will be me
Making me history

We all are suckers you see
God and Satan built the world around me

Maybe people will get their fill of pain
Leading the world of the insane

HEAVEN and HELL are raising cane
Because you all are the ones insane
Giving unto God undue pain

Arthur is only one to gain
God building more of His world
Again and again and again and again

If God had it to do over
He would build around me again and again
NO one else would listen to His plans

Mercy, Mercy

2010

I always thought I would like to have been
An angel of mercy

That's all wrong to wish for
People do not want an angel of Mercy!!!
They want Gods vengeance
Vengeance against all but themselves

People are nothing but Hell deserving sinners
People do not know nor believe this

If God directs His Perfect Judgments
Equally to all humans
America would be the first to be disciplined

What is God going to do to America??/
Blow it up?
Burn it up?
Make it fall in the ocean?
Or starve us out?
Like the world wishes

People should ask for Mercy from God
Not His vengeful judgments

If we want to see Gods judgment
Please visit the cemeteries
Counting all the dead receiving judgment
With their Mercy upon death.

In this life ask for mercy
Not Gods Perfect judgment
Cause each of us would perfectly
Go straight to Hell
Unless we are a prophet of His

I wished to be an angel of Mercy
I received no humanly acceptance

See Ya N Hell

April 27, 2010

I said we'll see you in Hell
Well I was partially right
It should have been
I am seeing you now in Hell
That is present tense

We are already in Hell
So I wasn't lying
Only presently misunderstood

We'll still see you in the Hell
Of this afterlife

The afterlife is what is usually meant
But I also mean Hell of this life

Hell is earth
If this isn't hell
Then no Hell exists in the afterlife

This life is Gods test
In order for us humans
To learn from God

Heaven and Hell certainly exists

Angel of Mercy in disguise says
See ya in Hell

The only way to fly
Is to be an angel with wings
That God is crazy about

See ya in Hell

Cowboys, Indians, Negroes, Whites

April 27, 2010

Early Americans were fighting for freedom
From England's rules
What was the Native Americans fighting for?
I bet it was freedom from American rule!!

Who was right?
Or was both right?
With might the winner?

Indians had to give up
Because might had too many bodies
For Indians to defeat

Were Indians truly free?

Indians were free until Americans took over.
Americans then hired black slaves
For room and board to till the land.
This way America could get freedom started through slavery.

The Civil War was fought for American Negro freedom.
Both sides of civil were Americans for freedom
Was one side civilly against American Freedom?
Or was it just a dispute being civilly divided on freedom?
I say civil was a major war for American freedom

Why weren't the other wars called civil
If they were for freedom also?
What war isn't civil?
What war is criminal?

Criminals aren't always prosecuted after war is over.
Because someone wins
Both sides of war usually have no remorse

Cowboys, Indians, Negros and Whites
Who was right?

Why can' people just get along?
The Civil War was fought over states rights

Does Jesus Need to be Forgave

Aug. 6, 2010

Does Jesus need to be forgiven?
For killing Himself on the cross?
He was 100% in charge
Of His crucifixion.

Being in charge of His death
He was 100% guilty of suicide
When He died from crucifixion
For forgiveness of our sins.

Jesus is God.
So He is always right.
Never needing to be forgiven
But what He did on the cross.
Was suicide, by human standards.

Most people are taught and believe
Suicide is unforgiven.
I don't know why suicide is unforgiven
It must be because
You are not alive
Being able to ask Jesus for forgiveness.

Who can forgive Jesus?
If He was wrong by us humans
For committing suicide
On the cross?

Does God ever forgive suicide?
Especially if He is at fault?
Although being the cause with no faults.
What isn't Jesus in charge of?
And how far do you take His perfection?

Satan Rules This Evil World

"The World" Brought to Its Knees

Aug. 6, 2010

So the world depends upon those boys!!!
We are the chosen ones!!!
Our father is in charge of ATOMIC bombs.
His number was next.
Back in 1945??

Our family causes wars.
And we can end them
ABRUPTLY
Jesus is always right
So who is to argue???

Satan blinds people's minds
He is this world's god.

Jesus wants to build His world around us
Much good is to come from those men
I ask God not to give others our pains.
Because I do not want the world to end that way
Happenings you would not wish upon a dog.

His boy's numbers was coming up
Around 1973.
The wars truce was signed,
The day before I was 18

We are God's inspiration of Life.
Lose Hymn and you all lose it all.
Why is God putting us men through this adversity?
Of course it's because He Loves Us
MORE THAN LIFE ITSELF

God disciplines the ones whom He loves

That is why people still cut our throats even after knowing
WHY, WHAT, WHERE, WHEN and WHO???!!!
People, It is soon gonna be too late.
It may be too late now.
The whole world depends on us men
I say to God: "BRING THE WORLD TO IT"S KNEES
God Almighty said to me, "ENOUGH IS ENOUGH

God is on Our Side

Aug. 7, 2010

Jesus made losers out of you all.
What does it feel like to be against someone?
That can never do any wrong?

You people thought you could do no wrong
Using God given power for lies, deceit, deception and greed
You are a bunch of fakes
Because God says so of your hatred and evil.

There are gangs, cliques, and organized crime
Here in Southern Illinois
They to me are called RICH REPUBLICAN CHRISTIANS
FOR CHRIST OUR LORD
Hatred is in their hearts for greed on their minds.

It is a buddy system of select pillars of the communities
They will always be right
In their rigged system of injustice they call justice
People are afraid of this buddy system
So nobody knows anything about nothing.

Some people just don't care of injustices
Some are misled just being a relative
Some are eager beavers
Being more wicked than Satan himself
People do around here what the Fallen Angels wouldn't do.

I lived in a place worse than hell
Well, the shoe is on the other foot now
Jesus set you up cause no would believe this story.
JESUS SET YOU ALL UP

Still people don't care
Being scared of Christian Republican scare tactics
People will gang up on God for evil personal gain.
Not knowing what they are doing.
Yet go to Church praying to him

This evil world is worse than Hell
If anyone cares to pay attention

Legion After Legion of Angels

2010

All Gods' angels can and will make mistakes.
All Gods' angels are perfect at recording human history.
None of Gods' angels miscount one single hair on a head.

All Gods' angels together can't count all my money.
King Arthur has too much money to count.
Computers burn up trying to count it.

Each hair on every body's head has a number.

WE all live in the past.
Everything has done happened before.
Nothing is new under the sun.
EVERYTHING BY GOD WAS DECIDED IN THE BEGINNING.
If God did not choose you, you don't go to Paradise.

People are gonna have to change their ways
Unless, they want to spend forever in the less desirable place.

Gods' angels don't forget the faithful servants.
They will forget the evil ones memories

Arthur is accusing the Church people of leading atheist lives.
Being atheist cause come Monday so called Christians
Forget God returning to the evil they and God despise.

All accusing the church of a lot of filler time
Teaching fairy tales about God, and believing them
Meaning deep down they are senseless of God

Is God mad?
Well not really. But it makes Him cry.
He makes us who we are????
God laughs at our foolishness.

Like I meant to say.
Angels have a perfect movie of all lives.

What else can make God Laugh and cry.
Let's not go there.
What silly people!!!???

Vengeance or Mercy???

Aug. 9, 2010

How many angels does God Need?
Repaying the world for evil?
He really needs only one angel.
It is called Destroyer or maybe an angel of Death.

How many angels does God have?
God commands more angels than He can numbers???
Yes! That's right, He can't even number them.
Destroyer or Death can take care of God's vengeance.
If God so desired.
God gives life so He can take life.

What are His Legions of angels doing?
They are seeing that the world doesn't'
Totally and instantly turn 100% evil.
They control everything.
Such as the animals, stars, weather and recording history.

Angels can and will make mistakes
But they are perfect in true history.

Does anyone want their life played on TV or radio?
It can be arranged to do so
Angels have very perfect memories.
No one gets anything over on an angel of God.

The angels are trying their best to keep score.
But Arthur has more money than angels can count.
Vengeance is the Lords.

What exactly do people want from God?
Is it REVENGE, VENGEANCE, JUDGEMENT, MERCY or money?

When God shows up will he be able to do anything right.
Without paying every one off with what they want?

Does God have enough money to pay them off?
WWJD WWJD WWJD WWJD WWJD

Use My Money

8/9/2010

The question is: Whose money are we gonna to use?

Someone had to give in
OK God you can use my money
To keep the fires in hell burning forever.

It is said: Strines have more money than Lynches can count.
King Arthur has more money than angels dare to count.
What money is left over not counted.
Arthur will donate to keep the fires in Hell burning forever.

No one in Heaven seems to care of money.
No one in Heaven claims to know a thing about money.
They don't know what I am talking about.

Please God use my money to burn hell eternally.

Why did God give it all to us?
Because nobody else could figure out what to do with it.

Some people just can't be trusted.

BURN IN HELL WITH MY MONEY

The End of Time

8/11/2010

The end of rhyme
Will mark the end of time

My poetry may be a little out of time
People betting every last dime.
I continue poetry rhyme.
Line by line
Whether or not the rhymes are in time

At least nine times I've given up rhyme
Caused from drinking wine from a vine.

Tonight I should have stayed drunk till nine.
So God could have buried me in pine.
From driving drunk, (A CRIME)

Kline bet every last dime
To steal, robbing us of even our lands lime.
Betting Art would not be healthy fine.
Wanting to fine the family every time
For every last dime.

Russell wanted to bury Jack, a brother of mine.
Russell is the one now surrounded by pine.
To God he looks fine
After paying his fine
For salvation through time

Arthur is continuing rhyme and time.
The clock is a ticking, Russell still whines

Will time continue without rhyme?
Who wins Kline or rhyme?
Who is really out of time?

The Great Temptation of Jesus

Aug. 23, 2010

Jesus fasted for 40 days and nights
Jesus then faced His Great Temptation from Satan
The temptation was: Ruler ship of this world

Satan is the ruler of this world of evil
It was and is Satan's to give
So back then if Jesus gave in to Satan
The whole shooting match between God Jesus and god Lucifer
Would have been over
And Jesus would not be able to offer forgiveness
All we humans would immediately be losers to sin

Of course the Great Temptation was real
If Satan doesn't rule
Then it was a fake temptation
And Jesus was a fake being a lie

After the temptation
The angels had to administer help to Him

Jesus who is God
Wants us humans to know
Satan is this world's ruler
And Satan won't let us forget it

If the Great Temptation wasn't real
We have missed a great theme of the Bible

Does Jesus have to draw us a picture
About the forces of good and evil?

It is impossible for Jesus to sin or for Satan to win

Rule The World Forever

Biography

I **Arthur Knackmus** pronounced (Knockmoose) was born at the hospital in Olney Illinois U.S.A. on Jan.29, 1955. I was the seventh of eight children born to Dale and Lorene (Mason) Knackmus. I am single never been married having no children. Although I haven't any offspring, I am well blessed with family members, having three brothers and four sisters. they have all been married. These siblings have a total of 19 children, 30 grand children, 6 great grand children, and 4 great great grand children. My mothers father grand pa Otto Mason had over 120 first cousins. On the Knackmus side we only have one first cousin.

Some of our distant Knackmus relatives migrated to America in the 1860's from Germany or Prussia. They took different spellings of Knackmus even though all three were brothers. The other spellings are Knakmuhs and Knackmuhs. These three families still live in and around West Salem Illinois. We have many distant relatives on the Knackmus side but few have the Knackmus name.

My parents raised me on a good sized farm south east of West Salem in the county of Edwards that's in South Eastern Illinois, U.S.A. Some years on the farm were productive other years it did not produce a profit. Lack of profits was due to being on the wrong side of the markets,floods, droughts, blights, field conditions, winds, insects, inflation and among other things four government grain embargoes of the 1970's. It is 2018 now and My brother has to deal with government tariffs, but the USA government gives him a subsidy payment to help make up the loss. (Welfare)

I, like the rest of my family clan claims to be of Christian faith, even though all of us do not agree who the Christian God and Creator is. To me it is Jesus. Nothing could exist without Him. I have not attended church for a long time but was taught about God and Christian values at a young age. The church of my youth was named The Moravian Church here in West Salem Illinois. The Moravian denomination is the oldest known church that separated from the Catholic Church back during the Reformation.

I attended a two year Junior College receiving an A.A.Science degree in coal mine technology graduating in 1982. The college is 20 miles south east of West Salem being called Wabash Valley College. It's in Mt. Carmel Illinois and it is known to have a great sports program nationally. I have been to several games through the years.

I have been disabled for sometime but did haul fresh drinking water to wells and cisterns at houses, along with helping on the farm. On the farm we would also cut a lot of timber to haul to the saw mill. We quit raising livestock many years ago.

I have other books that need to be published. They are "Memories to Burn" "Richer Than Money" and "Everybody Wanted to Win" The glory should go to God.

Many of my poems have been published by The International Library of Poetry. I was elected to their Hall of Fame in 1999. Famous Poets have published many. Poetry Fest has published many and I am also a Hall of Fame poet for them.

In the beginning I had no idea a book was being composed and I did not name any one of my books until it was almost completed. As of now I want to help other people namely students of all kinds in their process of learning. This book which God helped me greatly to complete and compose keeps the readers interested until it is finished really wanting more reading from this author. I have had critics review this book, they saying it is great.

I Arthur Knackmus pronounced (Knockmoose) was born at the hospital in Olney Illinois U.S.A. on Jan.29, 1955. I was the seventh of eight children born to Dale and Lorene (Mason) Knackmus. I am single never been married having no children. Although I haven't any offspring, I am well blessed with family members, having three brothers and four sisters. they have all been married. These siblings have a total of 19 children, 30 grand children, 6 great grand children, and 4 great great grand children. My mothers father grand pa Otto Mason had over 120 first cousins. On the Knackmus side we only have one first cousin.

Some of our distant Knackmus relatives migrated to America in the 1860's from Germany or Prussia. They took different spellings of Knackmus even though all three were brothers. The other spellings are Knakmuhs and Knackmuhs. These three families still live in and around West Salem Illinois. We have many distant relatives on the Knackmus side but few have the Knackmus name.

My parents raised me on a good sized farm south east of West Salem in the county of Edwards that's in South Eastern Illinois, U.S.A. Some years on the farm were productive other years it did not produce a profit. Lack of profits was due to being on the wrong side of the markets, floods, droughts, blights, field conditions, winds, insects, inflation and among other things four government grain embargoes of the 1970's. It is 2018 now and My brother has to deal with government tariffs, but the USA government gives him a subsidy payment to help make up the loss. (Welfare)

I, like the rest of my family clan claims to be of Christian faith, even though all of us do not agree who the Christian God and Creator is. To me it is Jesus. Nothing could exist without Him. I have not attended church for a long time but was taught about God and Christian values at a young age. The church of my youth was named The Moravian Church here in West Salem Illinois. The Moravian denomination is the oldest known church that separated from the Catholic Church back during the Reformation.

I attended a two year Junior College receiving an A.A.Science degree in coal mine technology graduating in 1982. The college is 20 miles south east of West Salem being called Wabash Valley College. It's in Mt. Carmel Illinois and it is known to have a great sports program nationally. I have been to several games through the years.

I have been disabled for sometime but did haul fresh drinking water to wells and cisterns at houses, along with helping on the farm. On the farm we would also cut a lot of timber to haul to the saw mill. We quit raising livestock many years ago.

I have other books that need to be published. They are"Memories to Burn" "Richer Than Money" and "Everybody Wanted to Win" The glory should go to God.

Many of my poems have been published by The International Library of Poetry. I was elected to their Hall of Fame in 1999. Famous Poets have published many. Poetry Fest has published many and I am also a Hall of Fame poet for them.

In the beginning I had no idea a book was being composed and I did not name any one of my books until it was almost completed. As of now I want to help other people namely students of all kinds in their process of learning. This book which God helped me greatly to complete and compose keeps the readers interested until it is finished really wanting more reading from this author. I have had critics review this book, they saying it is great.

Thanks!